661339

SIX
AMERICAN
POETS

SIX AMERICAN POETS

AN ANTHOLOGY
EDITED BY
JOEL CONARROE

WALT WHITMAN

EMILY DICKINSON

WALLACE STEVENS

WILLIAM CARLOS WILLIAMS

ROBERT FROST

LANGSTON HUGHES

Random House New York

Owing to limitations of space, permission credits for previously published material can be found on pages following Index of First Lines.

Photo Credits:

Photo of Emily Dickinson is reproduced courtesy of Amherst College Library by permission of the Trustees of Amherst College.

Photo of Robert Frost is reproduced courtesy of the Jones Library, Amherst College, by permission of the Trustees of Amherst College.

Photo of Wallace Stevens is reproduced courtesy of the Bettmann Archives.

Photo of Walt Whitman is reproduced courtesy of The William R. Perkins Library, Trent Collection.

Photo of William Carlos Williams courtesy of New Directions Publishing Corporation.

Library of Congress Cataloging-in-Publication Data

Six American poets / edited by Joel Conarroe.
p.   cm.
Contents: Walt Whitman—Emily Dickinson—Wallace Stevens—William Carlos Williams—Robert Frost—Langston Hughes.
ISBN 0-679-40689-1
1. American poetry. I. Conarroe, Joel.
PS586.S49 1991
811.008—dc20   91-15375

Manufactured in the United States of America

98765432

First Edition

For
Roslyn Schloss
Robert Savage
James Sgritto

ACKNOWLEDGMENTS

The idea of compiling an anthology of this sort was suggested to me by Brigitte Weeks, to whom, as I have been on other occasions, I am most grateful. I am also indebted, for kindnesses of various sorts along the way, to Patricia O'Sullivan, Jason Epstein, Jean McNutt, Helen Del Tredici, Cleo Tom, David Smith, Maryam Mohit, Melvin Thrash, Frank Doelger, Neil Baldwin, Peter Conn, Henry T. Lilly (my "old professor"), Brad Leithauser, and the estimable individuals whose names appear on the dedication page.

CONTENTS

INTRODUCTION

Breathes there a bard who isn't moved
When he finds his verse is understood
And not entirely disapproved
By his country and his neighborhood?
—ROBERT FROST,
"ON BEING CHOSEN POET OF VERMONT"

During my freshman year in college I had a literature teacher who unfailingly gave the impression that his very life depended on getting my classmates and me to appreciate what he so clearly loved. One morning, following a discussion of Whitman's Civil War poems, our usually ebullient mentor fell silent for several moments and then offered some advice I have valued ever since. "My young friends," he said, "I want to implore you to read some poetry every day for the rest of your lives—even if it's only a few lines!"

Nearly twenty years later I encountered this remarkable man at a class reunion and let him know that his apparently off-the-cuff suggestion had made a difference in my life. I was able to tell him that whatever stresses may disrupt my daily routine (and in New York, such disruptions are not unheard of), or cares (and car alarms) invade my sleep, I can count on the consolation of some memorable language singing in my mind—even if it's only a few lines. A daily exposure to poetry, in fact, not only offers me a welcome respite from certain aspects of contemporary life that are trivial or dispiriting (the unavoidable Muzak of reality) but also heightens my responsiveness to more enduring things that actually do merit close attention.

It is surely no mystery why readers return again and again to Shakespeare's sonnets, to Emily Dickinson's lyrics, and to other of what William Butler Yeats calls monuments of unaging intellect. Such works have an uncanny power to unlock the imaginative aspirations of those of us who are not ourselves gifted with creative genius. As C. S. Lewis so eloquently put it, "In reading literature one becomes a thousand men and women and yet remains oneself. Like a night sky in the Greek poem, I see with a myriad eyes, but it is still I who see. Here, as in worship, in love, in moral action, and in knowing, I transcend myself and am never more myself than when I do." Lifting us out of our ordinary routines, literature is able, paradoxically, to restore our truest selves.

To turn without delay to the monuments at hand: I can't offer any promises that the poets who make up this volume are necessarily going to negate the buzz and blare of contemporary life, or even that they will quicken a reader's pulse. I do believe, though, that anyone who settles in with these pages will almost certainly experience those flashes of insight, shocks of recognition, and feelings of well-being that transcendent art is capable of providing. What is required? Some engaging advice Italo Calvino offered readers of his fiction seems to me applicable also to anyone who picks up a volume of substantial poetry: "Concentrate. Dispel every other thought. Let the world around you fade." What is required, in short, is a willingness to let the music work its magic.

The music that invites your concentration (and collaboration) in this anthology is composed exclusively in the American idiom. Describing familiar landscapes (or cityscapes) and those who inhabit them, portraying local flora and fauna, and drawing on a shared storehouse of historical and cultural moments, American writers are uniquely equipped to provide us, their compatriots, with especially intense moments of recognition and revelation. These poets speak our language, literally and figuratively, though they clearly do so in different ways. There are in fact as many American voices as there are American writers, but what the artists in this book have in common is a familiarity with certain physical phenomena, an awareness of some pervasive myths and legends, and an innate understanding of our national character. They also share an intense response to the miracle of simply existing. Something the critic Randall Jarrell said about Wallace Stevens also applies, it seems to me, to the other poets in this book: "At the bottom of his poetry there is wonder and delight, the child's or animal's or savage's—man's—joy in his own existence, and thankfulness for it."

When I say that American poets speak with special force and resonance to their compatriots, I don't mean to imply that only homegrown writers are able to move American readers deeply; poetry is, after all, like music, a universal language. I do submit, however, that it is to the literature of his or her own country that even a cosmopolitan reader is likely to respond with the most "wonder and delight" and with the surest intuitive understanding. This has nothing at all to do with parochial flag-waving but is, rather, a question of the heightened capacity for response that is part of one's emotional and intellectual birthright.

While this collection, filled as it is with memorable work, should appeal to anyone already won over to American poetry, it is mainly designed for the general reader interested in being introduced, in an unhurried way, to some major voices: six such voices, to be precise. Although the United States can claim scores of inspiring poets, I have chosen to include extensive selections from a few central figures and not the too-brief sampling of pages from a much wider group that collections of this sort often comprise. "An editor," the statesman Adlai Stevenson once said, "is one who separates the wheat from the chaff and prints the chaff." I don't think, though, that any reader will find much chaff here. No anthology, of course, can begin to satisfy everyone (the possibilities for sins of commission *and* omission are endless), but I am persuaded that by joining the two monumental figures from our last century with four essential voices from this one, the collection you are holding will provide an introduction to the great feast of American poetry that is both satisfying and nourishing.

The poets who share these pages, I noticed after selecting them, fall into three pairs of nearly polar opposites. One pair is composed of the nineteenth-century originals. Walt Whitman, the most gregarious of individuals, was not in the least averse to self-promotion or even to reviewing his own books, whereas the reclusive Emily Dickinson ("I'm Nobody! Who are you?"), whose work was published only after her death, stands in the ranks of America's fascinating breed of literary "isolatos." The works of these influential contemporaries (who never met) clearly reflect their very different personalities.

A great democrat, Whitman thought it a poet's primary function to cheer up slaves and horrify despots—a nice variation on Saint Augustine's "Spare the lowly and strike down the proud."

The runaway slave came to my house and stopt outside,
I heard his motions crackling the twigs of the woodpile,
Through the swung half-door of the kitchen I saw him
    limpsy and weak,
And went where he sat on a log and led him in and
    assured him,
And brought water and fill'd a tub for his sweated body
    and bruis'd feet,
And gave him a room that enter'd from my own, and
    gave him some coarse clean clothes . . .

Determined to include everyone and everything in his huge free-verse structures, this admirer of Verdi composed soaring arias that contain many lines that are sublime—"I believe a leaf of grass is no less than the journeywork of the stars"—and others that are not—"Then courage, European revolter, revoltress!" (An early if inconsistent champion of nonsexist usage, the poet clearly had his heart in the right place even if some of his diction sounds decidedly curious today.)

Dickinson, by contrast, created perfectly ordered chamber pieces rather than vast operas; her art is one of compression.

Surgeons must be very careful
When they take the knife!
Underneath their fine incisions
Stirs the Culprit — *Life*!

The nearly two thousand concise lyrics that make up her letter to the world necessarily lack the spacious grandeur of Whitman's uninhibited revelations, but they display a sparkling epigrammatic precision. Whatever their differences, each of these writers, brilliant in an idiosyncratic way, exerted a powerful influence on generations of artists to follow.

William Carlos Williams, a Whitman-intoxicated physician in Rutherford, New Jersey, and Wallace Stevens, a reserved Hartford, Connecticut, insurance executive, form a second pair of disparate sensibilities. Williams, who spent much of his life taking care of working-class women and children, introduced an unembellished idiom into the texture of his verse. The language of America, he insisted, is not the language of England; he wanted to rescue poetry from European conventions of regular rhythm and rhyme, to translate the sometimes crude, often urgent, utterances of his unsophisticated neighbors into enduring art.

Is this the baby specialist?

Yes, but perhaps you mean my son,
can't you wait until   .   ?

I, I, I don't think it's brEAthin'

Williams was especially fascinated by the mundane details of ordinary suburban life that others found anything but literary—Stevens, in fact, used the word "anti-poetic" to describe this approach. "No ideas but in things," Williams proclaimed, a credo unsympathetic critics have misread to mean "No ideas." Because he was so scientifically impartial an observer, it was said against him that no one could possibly love anything as much as he loved *everything*.

> I walk back streets
> admiring the houses
> of the very poor:
> roof out of line with sides
> the yards cluttered
> with old chicken wire, ashes,
> furniture gone wrong;
> the fences and outhouses
> built of barrel-staves
> and parts of boxes, all,
> if I am fortunate,
> smeared a bluish green
> that properly weathered
> pleases me best
> of all colors.

Like Whitman, his spiritual father, Williams wanted both to record the miracle of the daily spectacle and to give a voice to his essentially inarticulate townspeople. His sharply focused work, free of artifice, is accessible even on a first hearing.

The more cosmopolitan Stevens, for his part, at least until the relatively straightforward work of his later years, was attracted by a more thickly orchestrated music, which is symbolic, witty, allusive—and elusive.

> People are not going
> To dream of baboons and periwinkles.
> Only, here and there, an old sailor,
> Drunk and asleep in his boots,
> Catches tigers
> In red weather.

"Even when you do not know what he is saying," Edmund Wilson observed, "you know that he is saying it well." The difference between Stevens's luxuriously loaded poetic vehicle and Williams's stripped-down model is evident in the contrast between a four-line Williams lyric, "El Hombre," printed below in italics, and Stevens's response to it, "Nuances of a Theme by Williams"—ten lines of free-wheeling embellishment.

> *It's a strange courage*
> *you give me ancient star:*
>
> *Shine alone in the sunrise*
> *toward which you lend no part!*

> I
> Shine alone, shine nakedly, shine like bronze,
> that reflects neither my face nor any inner part
> of my being, shine like fire, that mirrors nothing.

II

Lend no part to any humanity that suffuses
you in its own light.
Be not chimera of morning,
Half-man, half-star.
Be not an intelligence,
Like a widow's bird
Or an old horse.

Opening with the conversational "It's," Williams immediately establishes a simple connection between an isolated morning star and a speaker who is moved by its independence. This observer is clearly exhorting himself ("Shine alone") while praising the ancient star. There are no ambiguities here, no rhetorical flourishes.

The speaker in Stevens's incantatory variations, by contrast, denies any relation between man and star through a series of sensuous images. In Stevens everything is invariably likened or opposed to something else, and here the star is seen first in relation to bronze and fire (resonant inanimate objects), then to a "chimera" (a mythical fire-breathing monster), and finally, by a totally unexpected leap, to a widow's bird and an old horse (decidedly nonmythological domestic creatures). Like the aesthetically satisfying poem that contains it, the radiant star, offering "no part to any humanity," is an end in itself—art as its own excuse for being. Stevens's elaborate variations, with their negations and emphasis on impersonality, could hardly be less like the small, humane lyric that serves as their starting point and that ends as their subtext.

· · ·

For a final pair of voices, Robert Frost, the droll and sometimes disturbing recorder of New England farmscapes and Yankee voices, joins Langston Hughes, whose jazzy rhythms capture the vitality of urban life, especially in Harlem. Each of these artists gives us sharply rendered individuals who embody the values and tensions of a specific time and place, but in other ways their poetics are light years apart. Frost's pastoral narratives are inhabited by weather-wise men and women who sound as spontaneous as one's own neighbors, though in fact their talk falls with clocklike precision into regular meters:

> I'm góing oút to cléan the pásture spríng;
> I'll only stóp to ráke the léaves awáy
> (And wáit to wátch the wáter cléar, I máy):
> I shán't be góne lóng. — Yóu come tóo.

The poet, as a rebuke to Carl Sandburg, said he would as soon "play tennis with the net down" as write free verse.

Keeping his own net always at regulation height, Frost produced some of our century's most compelling verse. Even in his shorter lyrics, and certainly in his larger narratives, he engages our attention by presenting believable actors in dramatic situations, whether the old hired man who returns to a farm to die, the boy who swings on birches, or the traveler who simply stops to savor the beauty of a snow-filled woods. His Yankee voice has an unmistakable tang, but like all effective dramatists, Frost knows how to locate the precise tone and diction for the distinctive creatures of his imagination, those unlettered but seasoned folk who people his quintessentially American body of work.

> Out of the mud two strangers came
> And caught me splitting wood in the yard.
> And one of them put me off my aim
> By hailing cheerily "Hit them hard!"
> I knew pretty well why he dropped behind
> And let the other go on a way.
> I knew pretty well what he had in mind:
> He wanted to take my job for pay.

Langston Hughes's characters come from a quite different corner of American life. Urban, irreverent, alternately joyful and sorrowing, they give voice to a segment of society that has been underrepresented in our art. And where Frost's narratives generally unfold in an unhurried manner appropriate to the boundless acres they commemorate, Hughes's brief lyrics are nervous and full of abrupt shifts, like city life itself—and like the jazz riffs that inspired him.

> With his ebony hands on each ivory key
> He made that poor piano moan with melody.
>   O Blues!
> Swaying to and fro on his rickety stool
> He played that sad raggy tune like a musical fool.
>   Sweet Blues!
> Coming from a black man's soul.
>   O Blues!

His idiomatic lyrics, many of them, like this passage, based on the blues, put words around the fates of individuals who respond to life's inevitable disappointments with good-natured defiance. The irrepressible Alberta K. Johnson ("Madam to you"), whose streetwise monologues won't make anyone think of birch trees or snowy woods, is a case in point. Although she loses her man and a number of jobs and can't pay the rent, Madam brims with the high spirits and self-respect of a survivor. Like Frost's poor and unsentimental old farmers, she is impossible to resist.

> There's nothing foreign
> To my pedigree:
> Alberta K. Johnson —
> *American* that's me.

I'll end these introductory observations where they began—back in my college English classroom. I remember not only my old professor's injunction to make poetry an everyday part of our lives but also his advice about how to approach what for most of us was somewhat forbidding, though only because unfamiliar, as it turned out. I had assumed that a taste for poetry, anything but innate, required special training—like playing the saxophone or riding a camel. Our professor convinced us that anyone who can read has all the skill required to enjoy poetry, but that the more at home with the craft one becomes, the greater will be the satisfaction derived.

Our mentor also gave us some suggestions for enhancing the experience. He stressed that unlike most prose, poetry should be read, if not quite so deliberately as it is written, at least *lingeringly,* in a manner that allows one to savor its special music. It is also best read out loud for a full appreciation of verbal melodies and rhythmical modulations. A poem on the page is something like a musical score, waiting to be played. And like any good piece of music, it can be heard over and over until one is able to assert something like proprietary rights—until, that is, it becomes part of one's personal repertoire, like those songs we heard during adolescence and know by heart.

The poem that on first hearing may seem inscrutable will almost always shed some if not all of its mystery as one gets to know it better. E. A. Robinson described poetry as "language which tells us, through a more or less emotional reaction, something that cannot be said." Since much of this emotional power is communicated by rhythm, whether the work is conventionally structured or free of regular meter, hearing the music of the lines is a useful first step in apprehending what the poet is attempting to do. And I say "do" rather than "say" since exceptional works of art, unlike telephone bills, are not concerned with message units. They exist, instead, to put the best possible words around the unique experience of a creative imagination. Whenever W. H. Auden met a young person who said "I have important things to say," he offered no encouragement, but if the budding writer said "I like hanging around words, listening to what they say," he knew this might be a poet.

There are a few key questions to ask about any poem, the basic ones being simply who is speaking, who is being addressed, what is the occasion, and how is the sound related to the sense. Sometimes the speaker will be the poet, addressing us in his or her own voice, as when Whitman says "I shall be good health to you"; in other poems we overhear a speaker musing out loud. In still other instances—Frost's dramatic dialogues, for example—the poet functions as dramatist, creating characters through whom ideas—with which the poet may or may not be in sympathy—are expressed. The reader always serves as an unseen auditor, hearing or overhearing the combination of thought and emotion that gives rise to a particular sequence of words, artfully shaped to evoke a particular response.

The length and complexity of the poem help determine the nature of our participation. We settle into a long Whitman sequence the way we approach a movement of a symphony, responsive not only to individual moments but also to the cumulative effect. With Dickinson, though, the experience is more like a concert of short, self-contained songs, each with a sharp sense of closure. Stevens's meditative lyrics require a greater degree of intellectual collaboration than do, say, Williams's sharply focused vignettes. Both Frost and Hughes, to a large degree, call on us to be witnesses to the high drama enacted by the creatures of their imaginations. (A poem, Frost said, is a performance in words.) On a first reading one should listen closely to each of these poets to get the general picture, and then listen again. And again. There are no deadlines, no need to return this collection to a library. The experience should be savored.

Which is not to say that something is wrong if you don't take to all these writers. Readers occasionally need to be reminded to respect their own taste, their unique responses, and not to assume that an artist must be fine merely because others say so. We trust implicitly our impressions of friends and colleagues, and there are clearly reasons to respond intensely, perhaps even viscerally, to new acquaintances—even in a book. It is unlikely that any reader will relish all six of these artists equally—only an auctioneer, Oscar Wilde said, can be enthusiastic about all forms of art. You may even decide never to read another line by one or more of these poets, while enthusiastically seeking the collected works of others. My only recommendation is to give each a thorough hearing: with powerful poetry, familiarity invariably breeds respect.

For years, I now admit with some chagrin, I had reservations about Robert Frost, finding him conventional and excessively homespun in comparison with, say, T. S. Eliot, Marianne Moore, and others of his major contemporaries. The more I read his work, however, the greater was my regard, not only for his language and ironic humor but also for his tragic sense of life, which I had underestimated. I now think of him as Williams's equal, high praise in my particular hierarchy. Here is a dark lyric that took quite some time to win me over.

DESIGN

> I found a dimpled spider, fat and white,
> On a white heal-all, holding up a moth
> Like a white piece of rigid satin cloth —
> Assorted characters of death and blight
> Mixed ready to begin the morning right,
> Like the ingredients of a witches' broth —
> A snow-drop spider, a flower like a froth,
> And dead wings carried like a paper kite.

What had that flower to do with being white,
The wayside blue and innocent heal-all?
What brought the kindred spider to that height,
Then steered the white moth thither in the night?
What but design of darkness to appall? —
If design govern in a thing so small.

What a scary little dance of death this is! It is, of course,
ostensibly about nothing more significant than a couple of
insects, yet in Frost's artful handling we are exposed to a
dramatic moment that suggests something ominous about the
"design" of nature. The poem is a sonnet, its first section
setting up a situation and the final lines offering a comment
on that situation. ("A true sonnet," Frost said, "goes eight lines
and then takes a turn for the better or worse and goes six lines
more.") The work itself is a "thing so small," with its design
revealed by the orderly meter and rhyme, as well as by the
series of contrasts that gradually emerge—between whiteness
and darkness, life and death, innocence and depravity, morning
and night. All this in fourteen carefully plotted lines.

The situation could hardly be more ordinary: the speaker,
walking along a country road, notices a spider on a flower
holding a dead moth, a sight we've all seen. From the begin-
ning, though, his telling suggests that there is something more
than usually unsettling about this. For one thing, the spider is
"dimpled," "fat," and "white," words that taken together in
this context somehow sound obscene. The repetition of
"white," a word associated with purity, is clearly ironic, as is
the reference to "satin cloth," which suggests, among other
things, a bridal gown. Ironic too are the kite (a child's harmless

toy) and, of course, the incongruously named "heal-all," which, usually blue, has inexplicably turned white. There is cynicism in the phrase "mixed ready to begin the morning right," which conjures up a homey breakfast of fresh coffee and orange juice and not a ghastly little daybreak repast. "Froth," suggesting foaming at the mouth, reinforces the unwholesome atmosphere.

The speaker is moved to speculate about this depraved scene—depraved, at least, in his morbid telling—asking, for example, why the usually blue "heal-all" is an albino, and hence "kindred" to the murderous spider, and what agency "steered" the moth to its seemingly predestined liaison. The implication is that if some overriding natural design is responsible for so insignificant an event, what hope has any of us. This fatalistic point of view may express the poet's own sense of things during a period of personal despondency, but whether or not it does is less important than the fact that he makes us believe it does.

Whatever the possibly grim biographical implications, the poet could not resist engaging in wordplay—Frost liked to make language dance to the "whack of his quip." I had read the poem many times before I realized that "appall" has as its root meaning the idea of "making pale." This relates not only to the bleaching of the "blue and innocent heal-all," which becomes implicated in the death, but also to all the other references to white (and blight) that make up the poem's own design. I also realized, again only after many readings, that "govern" has a secondary meaning of "steer," which adds a final irony to the speaker's expression of revulsion. What, after all, has steered *him* to this grisly ballet? The poem, needless to say, gives the lie to those who regard Frost as merely a folksy recorder of rustic anecdotes.

There is obviously a good deal going on in these few lines (and between them), more than in many of the poems in this collection. A short lyric by Whitman, say, or by Williams would not generally lend itself to this sort of reading. Their meanings tend to lie closer to the surface, their language to be less formally structured—the designs, in short, are not so dense. I chose to annotate this sonnet precisely because it does invite detailed analysis. I think, though, that the questions raised here can be equally well applied to virtually any poem in the anthology—what is the occasion, how does the manner of the telling reinforce the matter at hand, and what, finally, are the effects on the reader?

Since this anthology is meant largely to delight, I'll end my comments not with so unsettling a work (though depictions of evil exert their own powerful fascination) but with a brief lyric that celebrates a different form of design, Williams's "The Red Wheelbarrow."

so much depends
upon

a red wheel
barrow

glazed with rain
water

beside the white
chickens

These four tiny stanzas, each in a shape suggesting a wheelbarrow, do several things that account for the poem's charm and popularity. First, we are presented a simple irrefutable fact—that a good deal of ordinary yard work depends upon a familiar implement. More significant, however, the speaker, clearly taking an aesthetic as well as a purely practical position, reminds us that much depends on the way we perceive seemingly ordinary patterns or designs—of color (red, white), texture (glaze), and spatial relationship. So much depends, too, on the way we read poems. A red wheelbarrow, a sculpturelike form created by human ingenuity, becomes part of its natural surrounding in a sharply focused still life the poet encourages us to see, as if for the first time, with our own eyes.

He does so, moreover, through a series of small surprises, created by the line breaks: modifiers (wheel, rain, white) are separated on the page from their nouns (barrow, water, chickens), thus requiring us to reconnect them with our eyes (and ears) and hence to participate in creating the small, harmless design in which, contrary to Robert Frost, "white" means neither innocence nor corruption but simply "white." These chickens in the rain, unlike the bleached-out heal-all, could not be more natural. Williams was always willing to call a spade a spade, or a wheelbarrow a wheelbarrow. There is rarely more than meets the eye in his work, but it is essential that the eye take in the much that is actually there. Close attention to the seemingly ordinary, which can turn out to be anything but ordinary, accounts for one of the undeniable pleasures of spending time with poetry.

. . .

"I know of nothing else but miracles," Whitman said. The six poets represented here, each a recorder of miracles, have all given me a great deal of pleasure over many years and continue to be stimulating company during otherwise uninspiring hours. My hope is that you too will find your spirits refreshed by their articulate presence, and that you will want to keep them close by as companionable sources of renewal and delight.

WALT WHITMAN

Walter Whitman liked to present himself not as a "dainty dolce affetuoso" (whatever that may be) but as "one of the roughs," a man more at home with unlettered laborers than with the "learned astronomers." Tall, bearded, and slow moving, he favored homespun suits and open-collared shirts without ties. "I wear my hat as I please," he wrote, "indoors or out." His usual form of greeting was a robust "Howdy!" Photographs reveal a jaunty fellow who appears to be self-assured and genial but whose blazing eyes suggest an intense drama taking place behind the seemingly easygoing exterior. Like Ernest Hemingway and Norman Mailer in our own century, "Walt" fashioned for himself a distinctive swaggering image, "turbulent, fleshly, sensual," a cocky public persona whose reality is sometimes reinforced by the work itself but at other times belied by passages revealing a complex sensibility that is anything but serene.

Born on rural Long Island in 1819 into a family that had been in America since the 1600s, Whitman died seventy-three years later in Camden, New Jersey, where he spent his final years as a semi-invalid, visited by admirers (including Oscar Wilde) who came from all over the world to meet him. (His house is now preserved as a museum.) Before this final sojourn his life had been remarkably peripatetic, starting with the earliest years, when his father, a house builder, moved frequently. By the time Walt was twelve and serving as an apprentice printer in Brooklyn, he had lived in a dozen different places.

As a teenager and as a young man he was something of a drifter, holding in rapid succession a mulligan stew of positions, including those of printer-journalist, reporter, and, intermittently, teacher. At thirty, having produced a mediocre temperance novel (which he claimed to have written in three days while drunk), as well as poems and editorials of no special distinction, and having served briefly as editor of several newspapers, including the influential Brooklyn *Daily Eagle,* he was named a special writer for the New Orleans *Crescent.* This Louisiana residency, his only extended period outside New York, later gave rise to the rumor (which he encouraged) that he was the father of several illegitimate children by a Creole mistress. Since no trace of these alleged children ever emerged and since, moreover, his only emotionally charged relationships were with working-class "comarados," the story is without merit.

The year 1855 stands as a red-letter date in American literature, for it is when the thirty-six-year-old poet published at his own expense a ninety-five-page "language experiment," made up of twelve untitled poems (and a long preface), called *Leaves of Grass*. On the title page, instead of the author's name, there was an engraved portrait of the poet, in shirtsleeves and wearing a hat tilted at a raffish angle. He would continue to revise and expand this book for the rest of his life—by the 1881 edition it had grown to 293 poems and 382 pages. The work, whose free, sweeping lines have the force of ocean breakers on his native Long Island shore, was unlike anything that had been published before, though its sources and antecedents can be discerned—the Bible, Homer, Shakespeare, Italian opera, and Ralph Waldo Emerson, among others.

"I was simmering, simmering, simmering," the poet said, "and Emerson brought me to a boil." Emerson, who in an 1844 essay, "The Poet," had called for an American bard, was enthusiastic and wrote what was to become perhaps the most famous blurb in literary history: "I find it the most extraordinary piece of wit and wisdom that America has yet contributed. . . . I greet you at the beginning of a great career." Whitman, who was not above such mischief, gave public exposure to Emerson's private letter and also wrote three glowing anonymous reviews of his own work, one of them opening with the words "An American bard at last!" ("The public is a thick-skinned beast," he said late in his life, "and you have to keep whacking away at its hide to let it know you're there.")

Not everyone shared Emerson's high opinion of *Leaves of Grass*. James Russell Lowell called it "a solemn humbug," John Greenleaf Whittier reportedly threw his copy into the fire, and William Dean Howells, the dean of American novelists, objected to the book's "preponderant beastliness." In fact,

Whitman was dismissed from a government clerkship by the Secretary of the Interior because of his "indecent" book, which was later banned in Boston. (A Boston reviewer said the poet must be "some escaped lunatic raving in pitiable delirium," and *The New York Times* called him a "half beast.") Today, what with the sort of literature that since Joyce's *Ulysses* and Lawrence's *Lady Chatterley's Lover* we take pretty much in stride, it may be difficult to see what all the fuss was about. In the mid-nineteenth century, however, when the mere mention of body parts was taboo, the sensuality of Whitman's "wild barbaric yawp," and especially his unabashed celebration of the human form, could hardly help but evoke hostility as well as admiration.

Through me forbidden voices,
Voices of sexes and lusts, voices veil'd and I remove the
    veil,
Voices indecent by me clarified and transfigur'd.

I do not press my fingers across my mouth,
I keep as delicate around the bowels as around the head
    and heart,
Copulation is no more rank to me than death is.

I believe in the flesh and the appetites,
Seeing, hearing, feeling, are miracles, and each part and tag
    of me is a miracle.

During the Civil War, by then in his forties and thus well beyond draft age, Whitman assumed the role of "Good Gray Poet," dressing wounds and comforting the disabled with his cheer and magnetism as a volunteer hospital worker in Washington, D.C. This fulfilling experience provided the source of some of his most moving lyrics, published as *Drum-Taps*, a collection that has inspired several contemporary composers, including Ned Rorem and John Adams, who have given the words evocative musical settings.

Open the envelope quickly,
O this is not our son's writing, yet his name is sign'd,
O a strange hand writes for our dear son, O stricken
    mother's soul!
All swims before her eyes, flashes with black, she catches
    the main words only,
Sentences broken, *gunshot wound in the breast, cavalry
    skirmish, taken to hospital,*
At present low, but will soon be better.

Whitman was also deeply affected by the death of Abraham Lincoln, a man he saw as embodying what is most noble about our country, "the sweetest, wisest soul of all my days and lands." It is fitting that the nation's greatest leader should have found his eulogist in our greatest poet.

My Captain does not answer, his lips are pale and still,
My father does not feel my arm, he has no pulse nor will,
The ship is anchor'd safe and sound, its voyage closed and
    done,
From fearful trip the victor ship comes in with object won;
    Exult O shores, and ring O bells!
      But I with mournful tread,
        Walk the deck my Captain lies,
        Fallen cold and dead.

Several paperback editions of Whitman are in print. For a well-edited hardback edition of the complete work (prose as well as poetry) I recommend the one-volume *Walt Whitman* edited by Justin Kaplan and published by the Library of America in 1982. For biographical information, two works are especially helpful: Justin Kaplan's *Walt Whitman: A Life* (Bantam, 1982) and Gay Wilson Allen's *The Solitary Singer: A Critical Biography of Walt Whitman* (New York University Press, 1967). See also Paul Zweig, *Walt Whitman: The Making of a Poet* (Basic Books, 1984).

I HEAR AMERICA SINGING

I hear America singing, the varied carols I hear,
Those of mechanics, each one singing his as it should be
    blithe and strong,
The carpenter singing his as he measures his plank or
    beam,
The mason singing his as he makes ready for work, or
    leaves off work,
The boatman singing what belongs to him in his boat, the
    deckhand singing on the steamboat deck,
The shoemaker singing as he sits on his bench, the hatter
    singing as he stands,
The wood-cutter's song, the ploughboy's on his way in the
    morning, or at noon intermission or at sundown,
The delicious singing of the mother, or of the young wife
    at work, or of the girl sewing or washing,
Each singing what belongs to him or her and to none else,
The day what belongs to the day — at night the party of
    young fellows, robust, friendly,
Singing with open mouths their strong melodious songs.

From SONG OF MYSELF

1

I celebrate myself, and sing myself,
And what I assume you shall assume,
For every atom belonging to me as good belongs to you.

I loafe and invite my soul,
I lean and loafe at my ease observing a spear of summer
    grass.

My tongue, every atom of my blood, form'd from this
    soil, this air,
Born here of parents born here from parents the same, and
    their parents the same,
I, now thirty-seven years old in perfect health begin,
Hoping to cease not till death.

Creeds and schools in abeyance,
Retiring back a while sufficed at what they are, but never
    forgotten,
I harbor for good or bad, I permit to speak at every
    hazard,
Nature without check with original energy.

6

A child said *What is the grass?* fetching it to me with full
    hands;
How could I answer the child? I do not know what it is
    any more than he.

I guess it must be the flag of my disposition, out of
    hopeful green stuff woven.

WALT WHITMAN 9

Or I guess it is the handkerchief of the Lord,
A scented gift and remembrancer designedly dropt,
Bearing the owner's name someway in the corners, that we
    may see and remark, and say *Whose?*

Or I guess the grass is itself a child, the produced babe of
    the vegetation.

Or I guess it is a uniform hieroglyphic,
And it means, Sprouting alike in broad zones and narrow
    zones,
Growing among black folks as among white,
Kanuck, Tuckahoe, Congressman, Cuff, I give them the
    same, I receive them the same.

And now it seems to me the beautiful uncut hair of
    graves.

Tenderly will I use you curling grass,
It may be you transpire from the breasts of young men,
It may be if I had known them I would have loved them,
It may be you are from old people, or from offspring
    taken soon out of their mothers' laps,
And here you are the mothers' laps.

This grass is very dark to be from the white heads of old
    mothers,
Darker than the colorless beards of old men,
Dark to come from under the faint red roofs of mouths.

O I perceive after all so many uttering tongues,
And I perceive they do not come from the roofs of
    mouths for nothing.

I wish I could translate the hints about the dead young
    men and women,
And the hints about old men and mothers, and the
    offspring taken soon out of their laps.

What do you think has become of the young and old
    men?
And what do you think has become of the women and
    children?

They are alive and well somewhere,
The smallest sprout shows there is really no death,
And if ever there was it led forward life, and does not
    wait at the end to arrest it,
And ceas'd the moment life appear'd.

All goes onward and outward, nothing collapses,
And to die is different from what any one supposed, and
    luckier.

8

The little one sleeps in its cradle,
I lift the gauze and look a long time, and silently brush
    away flies with my hand.

The youngster and the red-faced girl turn aside up the
    bushy hill,
I peeringly view them from the top.

The suicide sprawls on the bloody floor of the bedroom,
I witness the corpse with its dabbled hair, I note where the
    pistol has fallen.

The blab of the pave, tires of carts, sluff of boot-soles, talk
    of the promenaders,

The heavy omnibus, the driver with his interrogating
thumb, the clank of the shod horses on the granite
floor,
The snow-sleighs, clinking, shouted jokes, pelts of
snow-balls,
The hurrahs for popular favorites, the fury of rous'd mobs,
The flap of the curtain'd litter, a sick man inside borne to
the hospital,
The meeting of enemies, the sudden oath, the blows and
fall,
The excited crowd, the policeman with his star quickly
working his passage to the centre of the crowd,
The impassive stones that receive and return so many
echoes,
What groans of over-fed or half-starv'd who fall sunstruck
or in fits,
What exclamations of women taken suddenly who hurry
home and give birth to babes,
What living and buried speech is always vibrating here,
what howls restrain'd by decorum,
Arrests of criminals, slights, adulterous offers made,
acceptances, rejections with convex lips,
I mind them or the show or resonance of them — I come
and I depart.

10

Alone far in the wilds and mountains I hunt,
Wandering amazed at my own lightness and glee,
In the late afternoon choosing a safe spot to pass the night,
Kindling a fire and broiling the fresh-kill'd game,
Falling asleep on the gather'd leaves with my dog and gun
by my side.

The Yankee clipper is under her sky-sails, she cuts the
    sparkle and scud,
My eyes settle the land, I bend at her prow or shout
    joyously from the deck.

The boatmen and clam-diggers arose early and stopt for
    me,
I tuck'd my trowser-ends in my boots and went and had a
    good time;
You should have been with us that day round the
    chowder-kettle.

I saw the marriage of the trapper in the open air in the far
    west, the bride was a red girl,
Her father and his friends sat near cross-legged and dumbly
    smoking, they had moccasins to their feet and large
    thick blankets hanging from their shoulders,
On a bank lounged the trapper, he was drest mostly in
    skins, his luxuriant beard and curls protected his neck,
    he held his bride by the hand,
She had long eyelashes, her head was bare, her coarse
    straight locks descended upon her voluptuous limbs
    and reach'd to her feet.

The runaway slave came to my house and stopt outside,
I heard his motions crackling the twigs of the woodpile,
Through the swung half-door of the kitchen I saw him
    limpsy and weak,
And went where he sat on a log and led him in and
    assured him,
And brought water and fill'd a tub for his sweated body
    and bruis'd feet,
And gave him a room that enter'd from my own, and
    gave him some coarse clean clothes,

And remember perfectly well his revolving eyes and his
    awkwardness,
And remember putting plasters on the galls of his neck and
    ankles;
He staid with me a week before he was recuperated and
    pass'd north,
I had him sit next me at table, my fire-lock lean'd in the
    corner.

11

Twenty-eight young men bathe by the shore,
Twenty-eight young men and all so friendly;
Twenty-eight years of womanly life and all so lonesome.

She owns the fine house by the rise of the bank,
She hides handsome and richly drest aft the blinds of the
    window.

Which of the young men does she like the best?
Ah the homeliest of them is beautiful to her.

Where are you off to, lady? for I see you,
You splash in the water there, yet stay stock still in your
    room.

Dancing and laughing along the beach came the
    twenty-ninth bather,
The rest did not see her, but she saw them and loved
    them.

The beards of the young men glisten'd with wet, it ran
    from their long hair,
Little streams pass'd all over their bodies.

An unseen hand also pass'd over their bodies,
It descended tremblingly from their temples and ribs.

The young men float on their backs, their white bellies
    bulge to the sun, they do not ask who seizes fast to
    them,
They do not know who puffs and declines with pendant
    and bending arch,
They do not think whom they souse with spray.

24

Walt Whitman, a kosmos, of Manhattan the son,
Turbulent, fleshy, sensual, eating, drinking and breeding,
No sentimentalist, no stander above men and women or
    apart from them,
No more modest than immodest.

Unscrew the locks from the doors!
Unscrew the doors themselves from their jambs!

Whoever degrades another degrades me,
And whatever is done or said returns at last to me.

Through me the afflatus surging and surging, through me
    the current and index.
I speak the pass-word primeval, I give the sign of
    democracy,
By God! I will accept nothing which all cannot have their
    counterpart of on the same terms.

Through me many long dumb voices,
Voices of the interminable generations of prisoners and
    slaves,
Voices of the diseas'd and despairing and of thieves and
    dwarfs,

Voices of cycles of preparation and accretion,
And of the threads that connect the stars, and of wombs
     and of the father-stuff,
And of the rights of them the others are down upon,
Of the deform'd, trivial, flat, foolish, despised,
Fog in the air, beetles rolling balls of dung.

Through me forbidden voices,
Voices of sexes and lusts, voices veil'd and I remove the
     veil,
Voices indecent by me clarified and transfigur'd.

I do not press my fingers across my mouth,
I keep as delicate around the bowels as around the head
     and heart,
Copulation is no more rank to me than death is.

I believe in the flesh and the appetites,
Seeing, hearing, feeling, are miracles, and each part and tag
     of me is a miracle.

Divine am I inside and out, and I make holy whatever I
     touch or am touch'd from,
The scent of these arm-pits aroma finer than prayer,
This head more than churches, bibles, and all the creeds.

If I worship one thing more than another it shall be the
     spread of my own body, or any part of it,
Translucent mould of me it shall be you!
Shaded ledges and rests it shall be you! . . .

26
Now I will do nothing but listen,
To accrue what I hear into this song, to let sounds
     contribute toward it.

I hear bravuras of birds, bustle of growing wheat, gossip
of flames, clack of sticks cooking my meals,
I hear the sound I love, the sound of the human voice,
I hear all sounds running together, combined, fused or
following,
Sounds of the city and sounds out of the city, sounds of
the day and night,
Talkative young ones to those that like them, the loud
laugh of work-people at their meals,
The angry base of disjointed friendship, the faint tones of
the sick,
The judge with hands tight to the desk, his pallid lips
pronouncing a death-sentence,
The heave'e'yo of stevedores unlading ships by the
wharves, the refrain of the anchor-lifters,
The ring of alarm-bells, the cry of fire, the whirr of
swift-streaking engines and hose-carts with
premonitory tinkles and color'd lights,
The steam-whistle, the solid roll of the train of
approaching cars,
The slow march play'd at the head of the association
marching two and two,
(They go to guard some corpse, the flag-tops are draped
with black muslin.)

I hear the violoncello, ('tis the young man's heart's
complaint,)
I hear the key'd cornet, it glides quickly in through my
ears,
It shakes mad-sweet pangs through my belly and breast.

I hear the chorus, it is a grand opera,
Ah this indeed is music — this suits me.

A tenor large and fresh as the creation fills me,
The orbic flex of his mouth is pouring and filling me full.

I hear the train'd soprano (what work with hers is this?)
The orchestra whirls me wider than Uranus flies,
It wrenches such ardors from me I did not know I
  possess'd them,
It sails me, I dab with bare feet, they are lick'd by the
  indolent waves,
I am cut by bitter and angry hail, I lose my breath,
Steep'd amid honey'd morphine, my windpipe throttled in
  fakes of death,
At length let up again to feel the puzzle of puzzles,
And that we call Being.

31

I believe a leaf of grass is no less than the journey-work of
  the stars,
And the pismire is equally perfect, and a grain of sand, and
  the egg of the wren,
And the tree-toad is a chef-d'œuvre for the highest,
And the running blackberry would adorn the parlors of
  heaven,
And the narrowest hinge in my hand puts to scorn all
  machinery,
And the cow crunching with depress'd head surpasses any
  statue,
And a mouse is miracle enough to stagger sextillions of
  infidels. . . .

I think I could turn and live with animals, they are so
    placid and self-contain'd,
I stand and look at them long and long.

They do not sweat and whine about their condition,
They do not lie awake in the dark and weep for their sins,
They do not make me sick discussing their duty to God,
Not one is dissatisfied, not one is demented with the mania
    of owning things,
Not one kneels to another, nor to his kind that lived
    thousands of years ago,
Not one is respectable or unhappy over the whole
    earth. . . .

. . . I understand the large hearts of heroes,
The courage of present times and all times,
How the skipper saw the crowded and rudderless wreck of
    the steam-ship, and Death chasing it up and down the
    storm,
How he knuckled tight and gave not back an inch, and
    was faithful of days and faithful of nights,
And chalk'd in large letters on a board, *Be of good cheer,
we will not desert you;*
How he follow'd with them and tack'd with them three
    days and would not give it up,
How he saved the drifting company at last,
How the lank loose-gown'd women look'd when boated
    from the side of their prepared graves,
How the silent old-faced infants and the lifted sick, and
    the sharp-lipp'd unshaved men;

All this I swallow, it tastes good, I like it well, it becomes
    mine,
I am the man, I suffer'd, I was there.

The disdain and calmness of martyrs,
The mother of old, condemn'd for a witch, burnt with dry
    wood, her children gazing on,
The hounded slave that flags in the race, leans by the
    fence, blowing, cover'd with sweat,
The twinges that sting like needles his legs and neck, the
    murderous buckshot and the bullets,
All these I feel or am.

I am the hounded slave, I wince at the bite of the dogs,
Hell and despair are upon me, crack and again crack the
    marksmen,
I clutch the rails of the fence, my gore dribs, thinn'd with
    the ooze of my skin,
I fall on the weeds and stones,
The riders spur their unwilling horses, haul close,
Taunt my dizzy ears and beat me violently over the head
    with whip-stocks.

Agonies are one of my changes of garments,
I do not ask the wounded person how he feels, I myself
    become the wounded person,
My hurts turn livid upon me as I lean on a cane and
    observe.

I am the mash'd fireman with breast-bone broken,
Tumbling walls buried me in their debris,
Heat and smoke I inspired, I heard the yelling shouts of
    my comrades,

I heard the distant click of their picks and shovels,
They have clear'd the beams away, they tenderly lift me
	forth.

I lie in the night air in my red shirt, the pervading hush is
	for my sake,
Painless after all I lie exhausted but not so unhappy,
White and beautiful are the faces around me, the heads are
	bared of their fire-caps,
The kneeling crowd fades with the light of the torches.

Distant and dead resuscitate,
They show as the dial or move as the hands of me, I am
	the clock myself.

I am an old artillerist, I tell of my fort's bombardment,
I am there again.

Again the long roll of the drummers,
Again the attacking cannon, mortars,
Again to my listening ears the cannon responsive.

I take part, I see and hear the whole,
The cries, curses, roar, the plaudits for well-aim'd shots,
The ambulanza slowly passing trailing its red drip,
Workmen searching after damages, making indispensable
	repairs,
The fall of grenades through the rent roof, the fan-shaped
	explosion,
The whizz of limbs, heads, stone, wood, iron, high in the
	air.

Again gurgles the mouth of my dying general, he
	furiously waves with his hand,
He gasps through the clot *Mind not me — mind — the
entrenchments.*

Would you hear of an old-time sea-fight?
Would you learn who won by the light of the moon and
    stars?
List to the yarn, as my grandmother's father the sailor told
    it to me.

Our foe was no skulk in his ship I tell you, (said he,)
His was the surly English pluck, and there is no tougher
    or truer, and never was, and never will be;
Along the lower'd eve he came horribly raking us.

We closed with him, the yards entangled, the cannon
    touch'd,
My captain lash'd fast with his own hands.

We had receiv'd some eighteen pound shots under the
    water,
On our lower-gun-deck two large pieces had burst at the
    first fire, killing all around and blowing up overhead.

Fighting at sun-down, fighting at dark,
Ten o'clock at night, the full moon well up, our leaks on
    the gain, and five feet of water reported,
The master-at-arms loosing the prisoners confined in the
    after-hold to give them a chance for themselves.

The transit to and from the magazine is now stopt by the
    sentinels,
They see so many strange faces they do not know whom
    to trust.

Our frigate takes fire,
The other asks if we demand quarter?
If our colors are struck and the fighting done?

Now I laugh content, for I hear the voice of my little
    captain,
We have not struck, he composedly cries, *we have just begun
    our part of the fighting.*

Only three guns are in use,
One is directed by the captain himself against the enemy's
    mainmast,
Two well serv'd with grape and canister silence his
    musketry and clear his decks.

The tops alone second the fire of this little battery,
    especially the main-top,
They hold out bravely during the whole of the action.

Not a moment's cease,
The leaks gain fast on the pumps, the fire eats toward the
    powder-magazine.

One of the pumps has been shot away, it is generally
    thought we are sinking.

Serene stands the little captain,
He is not hurried, his voice is neither high nor low,
His eyes give more light to us than our battle-lanterns.

Toward twelve there in the beams of the moon they
    surrender to us.

52

The spotted hawk swoops by and accuses me, he complains
    of my gab and my loitering.

I too am not a bit tamed, I too am untranslatable,
I sound my barbaric yawp over the roofs of the world.

WALT WHITMAN   23

The last scud of day holds back for me,
It flings my likeness after the rest and true as any on the
    shadow'd wilds,
It coaxes me to the vapor and the dusk.

I depart as air, I shake my white locks at the runaway sun,
I effuse my flesh in eddies, and drift it in lacy jags.

I bequeath myself to the dirt to grow from the grass I
    love,
If you want me again look for me under your boot-soles.

You will hardly know who I am or what I mean,
But I shall be good health to you nevertheless,
And filter and fibre your blood.

Failing to fetch me at first keep encouraged,
Missing me one place search another,
I stop somewhere waiting for you.

From I SING THE BODY ELECTRIC

I

I sing the body electric,
The armies of those I love engirth me and I engirth them,
They will not let me off till I go with them, respond to
    them,
And discorrupt them, and charge them full with the charge
    of the soul.

Was it doubted that those who corrupt their own bodies
    conceal themselves?
And if those who defile the living are as bad as they who
    defile the dead?
And if the body does not do fully as much as the soul?
And if the body were not the soul, what is the soul?

I have perceiv'd that to be with those I like is enough,
To stop in company with the rest at evening is enough,
To be surrounded by beautiful, curious, breathing,
     laughing flesh is enough,
To pass among them or touch any one, or rest my arm
     ever so lightly round his or her neck for a moment,
     what is this then?
I do not ask any more delight, I swim in it as in a sea.

There is something in staying close to men and women
     and looking on them, and in the contact and odor of
     them, that pleases the soul well,
All things please the soul, but these please the soul well.

A man's body at auction,
(For before the war I often go to the slave-mart and
     watch the sale,)
I help the auctioneer, the sloven does not half know his
     business.

Gentlemen look on this wonder,
Whatever the bids of the bidders they cannot be high
     enough for it,
For it the globe lay preparing quintillions of years without
     one animal or plant,
For it the revolving cycles truly and steadily roll'd.

In this head the all-baffling brain,
In it and below it the makings of heroes.

Examine these limbs, red, black, or white, they are
     cunning in tendon and nerve,
They shall be script that you may see them.

Exquisite senses, life-lit eyes, pluck, volition,
Flakes of breast-muscle, pliant backbone and neck, flesh not
    flabby, good-sized arms and legs,
And wonders within there yet.

Within there runs blood,
The same old blood! the same red-running blood!
There swells and jets a heart, there all passions, desires,
    reachings, aspirations,
(Do you think they are not there because they are not
    express'd in parlors and lecture-rooms?)

This is not only one man, this the father of those who
    shall be fathers in their turns,
In him the start of populous states and rich republics,
Of him countless immortal lives with countless
    embodiments and enjoyments.

How do you know who shall come from the offspring of
    his offspring through the centuries?
(Who might you find you have come from yourself, if
    you could trace back through the centuries?)

ONCE I PASS'D THROUGH A POPULOUS CITY

Once I pass'd through a populous city imprinting my brain
    for future use with its shows, architecture, customs,
    traditions,
Yet now of all that city I remember only a woman I
    casually met there who detain'd me for love of me,
Day by day and night by night we were together — all
    else has long been forgotten by me,
I remember I say only that woman who passionately clung
    to me,

Again we wander, we love, we separate again,
Again she holds me by the hand, I must not go,
I see her close beside me with silent lips sad and tremulous.

I Heard You Solemn-Sweet Pipes of the Organ

I heard you solemn-sweet pipes of the organ as last Sunday
    morn I pass'd the church,
Winds of autumn, as I walk'd the woods at dusk I heard
    your long-stretch'd sighs up above so mournful,
I heard the perfect Italian tenor singing at the opera, I
    heard the soprano in the midst of the quartet singing;
Heart of my love! you too I heard murmuring low
    through one of the wrists around my head,
Heard the pulse of you when all was still ringing little
    bells last night under my ear.

As Adam Early in the Morning

As Adam early in the morning,
Walking forth from the bower refresh'd with sleep,
Behold me where I pass, hear my voice, approach,
Touch me, touch the palm of your hand to my body as I
    pass,
Be not afraid of my body.

Recorders Ages Hence

Recorders ages hence,
Come, I will take you down underneath this impassive
    exterior, I will tell you what to say of me,

Publish my name and hang up my picture as that of the
  tenderest lover,
The friend the lover's portrait, of whom his friend his
  lover was fondest,
Who was not proud of his songs, but of the measureless
  ocean of love within him, and freely pour'd it forth,
Who often walk'd lonesome walks thinking of his dear
  friends, his lovers,
Who pensive away from one he lov'd often lay sleepless
  and dissatisfied at night,
Who knew too well the sick, sick dread lest the one he
  lov'd might secretly be indifferent to him,
Whose happiest days were far away through fields, in
  woods, on hills, he and another wandering hand in
  hand, they twain apart from other men,
Who oft as he saunter'd the streets curv'd with his arm the
  shoulder of his friend, while the arm of his friend
  rested upon him also.

I Saw in Louisiana a Live-Oak Growing

I saw in Louisiana a live-oak growing,
All alone stood it and the moss hung down from the
  branches,
Without any companion it grew there uttering joyous
  leaves of dark green,
And its look, rude, unbending, lusty, made me think of
  myself,
But I wonder'd how it could utter joyous leaves standing
  alone there without its friend near, for I knew I
  could not,
And I broke off a twig with a certain number of leaves
  upon it, and twined around it a little moss,

And brought it away, and I have placed it in sight in my
    room,
It is not needed to remind me as of my own dear friends,
(For I believe lately I think of little else than of them,)
Yet it remains to me a curious token, it makes me think
    of manly love;
For all that, and though the live-oak glistens there in
    Louisiana solitary in a wide flat space,
Uttering joyous leaves all its life without a friend a lover
    near,
I know very well I could not.

To a Stranger

Passing stranger! you do not know how longingly I look
    upon you,
You must be he I was seeking, or she I was seeking, (it
    comes to me as of a dream,)
I have somewhere surely lived a life of joy with you,
All is recall'd as we flit by each other, fluid, affectionate,
    chaste, matured,
You grew up with me, were a boy with me or a girl with
    me,
I ate with you and slept with you, your body has become
    not yours only nor left my body mine only,
You give me the pleasure of your eyes, face, flesh, as we
    pass, you take of my beard, breast, hands, in return,
I am not to speak to you, I am to think of you when I sit
    alone or wake at night alone,
I am to wait, I do not doubt I am to meet you again,
I am to see to it that I do not lose you.

When I Peruse the Conquer'd Fame

When I peruse the conquer'd fame of heroes and the
    victories of mighty generals, I do not envy the
    generals,
Nor the President in his Presidency, nor the rich in his
    great house,
But when I hear of the brotherhood of lovers, how it was
    with them,
How together through life, through dangers, odium,
    unchanging, long and long,
Through youth and through middle and old age, how
    unfaltering, how affectionate and faithful they were,
Then I am pensive — I hastily walk away fill'd with the
    bitterest envy.

Sometimes with One I Love

Sometimes with one I love I fill myself with rage for fear
    I effuse unreturn'd love,
But now I think there is no unreturn'd love, the pay is
    certain one way or another,
(I loved a certain person ardently and my love was not
    return'd,
Yet out of that I have written these songs.)

Out of the Cradle Endlessly Rocking

Out of the cradle endlessly rocking,
Out of the mocking-bird's throat, the musical shuttle,
Out of the Ninth-month midnight,
Over the sterile sands and the fields beyond, where the
    child leaving his bed wander'd alone, bareheaded,
    barefoot,

Down from the shower'd halo,
Up from the mystic play of shadows twining and twisting
    as if they were alive,
Out from the patches of briers and blackberries,
From the memories of the bird that chanted to me,
From your memories sad brother, from the fitful risings
    and fallings I heard,
From under that yellow half-moon late-risen and swollen
    as if with tears,
From those beginning notes of yearning and love there in
    the mist,
From the thousand responses of my heart never to cease,
From the myriad thence-arous'd words,
From the word stronger and more delicious than any,
From such as now they start the scene revisiting,
As a flock, twittering, rising, or overhead passing,
Borne hither, ere all eludes me, hurriedly,
A man, yet by these tears a little boy again,
Throwing myself on the sand, confronting the waves,
I, chanter of pains and joys, uniter of here and hereafter,
Taking all hints to use them, but swiftly leaping beyond
    them,
A reminiscence sing.

Once Paumanok,
When the lilac-scent was in the air and Fifth-month grass
    was growing,
Up this seashore in some briers,
Two feather'd guests from Alabama, two together,
And their nest, and four light-green eggs spotted with
    brown,
And every day the he-bird to and fro near at hand,

And every day the she-bird crouch'd on her nest, silent,
    with bright eyes,
And every day I, a curious boy, never too close, never
    disturbing them,
Cautiously peering, absorbing, translating.

Shine! shine! shine!
Pour down your warmth, great sun!
While we bask, we two together.

Two together!
Winds blow south, or winds blow north,
Day come white, or night come black,
Home, or rivers and mountains from home,
Singing all time, minding no time,
While we two keep together.

Till of a sudden,
May-be kill'd, unknown to her mate,
One forenoon the she-bird crouch'd not on the nest,
Nor return'd that afternoon, nor the next,
Nor ever appear'd again.

And thenceforward all summer in the sound of the sea,
And at night under the full of the moon in calmer
    weather,
Over the hoarse surging of the sea,
Or flitting from brier to brier by day,
I saw, I heard at intervals the remaining one, the he-bird,
The solitary guest from Alabama.

Blow! blow! blow!
Blow up sea-winds along Paumanok's shore;
I wait and I wait till you blow my mate to me.

Yes, when the stars glisten'd,
All night long on the prong of a moss-scallop'd stake,
Down almost amid the slapping waves,
Sat the lone singer wonderful causing tears.

He call'd on his mate,
He pour'd forth the meanings which I of all men know.

Yes my brother I know,
The rest might not, but I have treasur'd every note,
For more than once dimly down to the beach gliding,
Silent, avoiding the moonbeams, blending myself with the
    shadows,
Recalling now the obscure shapes, the echoes, the sounds
    and sights after their sorts,
The white arms out in the breakers tirelessly tossing,
I, with bare feet, a child, the wind wafting my hair,
Listen'd long and long.

Listen'd to keep, to sing, now translating the notes,
Following you my brother.

Soothe! soothe! soothe!
Close on its wave soothes the wave behind,
And again another behind embracing and lapping, every one
    close,
But my love soothes not me, not me.

Low hangs the moon, it rose late,
It is lagging — O I think it is heavy with love, with love.

O madly the sea pushes upon the land,
With love, with love.

O night! do I not see my love fluttering out among the
     breakers?
What is that little black thing I see there in the white?

Loud! loud! loud!
Loud I call to you, my love!

High and clear I shoot my voice over the waves,
Surely you must know who is here, is here,
You must know who I am, my love.

Low-hanging moon!
What is that dusky spot in your brown yellow?
O it is the shape, the shape of my mate!
O moon do not keep her from me any longer.

Land! land! O land!
Whichever way I turn, O I think you could give me my mate
     back again if you only would,
For I am almost sure I see her dimly whichever way I look.

O rising stars!
Perhaps the one I want so much will rise, will rise with some
     of you.

O throat! O trembling throat!
Sound clearer through the atmosphere!
Pierce the woods, the earth,
Somewhere listening to catch you must be the one I want.

Shake out carols!
Solitary here, the night's carols!
Carols of lonesome love! death's carols!
Carols under that lagging, yellow, waning moon!
O under that moon where she droops almost down into the sea!
O reckless despairing carols.

But soft! sink low!
Soft! let me just murmur,
And do you wait a moment you husky-nois'd sea,
For somewhere I believe I heard my mate responding to me,
So faint, I must be still, be still to listen,
But not altogether still, for then she might not come
        immediately to me.

Hither my love!
Here I am! here!
With this just-sustain'd note I announce myself to you,
This gentle call is for you my love, for you.

Do not be decoy'd elsewhere,
That is the whistle of the wind, it is not my voice,
That is the fluttering, the fluttering of the spray,
Those are the shadows of leaves.

O darkness! O in vain!
O I am very sick and sorrowful.

O brown halo in the sky near the moon, drooping upon the
        sea!
O troubled reflection in the sea!
O throat! O throbbing heart!
And I singing uselessly, uselessly all the night.

O past! O happy life! O songs of joy!
In the air, in the woods, over fields,
Loved! loved! loved! loved! loved!
But my mate no more, no more with me!
We two together no more.

The aria sinking,
All else continuing, the stars shining,

The winds blowing, the notes of the bird continuous echoing,
With angry moans the fierce old mother incessantly moaning,
On the sands of Paumanok's shore gray and rustling,
The yellow half-moon enlarged, sagging down, drooping, the face of the sea almost touching,
The boy ecstatic, with his bare feet the waves, with his hair the atmosphere dallying,
The love in the heart long pent, now loose, now at last tumultuously bursting,
The aria's meaning, the ears, the soul, swiftly depositing,
The strange tears down the cheeks coursing,
The colloquy there, the trio, each uttering,
The undertone, the savage old mother incessantly crying,
To the boy's soul's questions sullenly timing, some drown'd secret hissing,
To the outsetting bard.

Demon or bird! (said the boy's soul,)
Is it indeed toward your mate you sing? or is it really to me?
For I, that was a child, my tongue's use sleeping, now I have heard you,
Now in a moment I know what I am for, I awake,
And already a thousand singers, a thousand songs, clearer, louder and more sorrowful than yours,
A thousand warbling echoes have started to life within me, never to die.

O you singer solitary, singing by yourself, projecting me,
O solitary me listening, never more shall I cease perpetuating you,
Never more shall I escape, never more the reverberations,

Never more the cries of unsatisfied love be absent from
    me,
Never again leave me to be the peaceful child I was before
    what there in the night,
By the sea under the yellow and sagging moon,
The messenger there arous'd, the fire, the sweet hell within,
The unknown want, the destiny of me.

O give me the clew! (it lurks in the night here
    somewhere,)
O if I am to have so much, let me have more!

A word then, (for I will conquer it,)
The word final, superior to all,
Subtle, sent up — what is it? — I listen;
Are you whispering it, and have been all the time, you
    sea-waves?
Is that it from your liquid rims and wet sands?

Whereto answering, the sea,
Delaying not, hurrying not,
Whisper'd me through the night, and very plainly before
    daybreak,
Lisp'd to me the low and delicious word death,
And again death, death, death, death,
Hissing melodious, neither like the bird nor like my
    arous'd child's heart,
But edging near as privately for me rustling at my feet,
Creeping thence steadily up to my ears and laving me
    softly all over,
Death, death, death, death, death.

Which I do not forget,
But fuse the song of my dusky demon and brother,

That he sang to me in the moonlight on Paumanok's gray
    beach,
With the thousand responsive songs at random,
My own songs awaked from that hour,
And with them the key, the word up from the waves,
The word of the sweetest song and all songs,
That strong and delicious word which, creeping to my
    feet,
(Or like some old crone rocking the cradle, swathed in
    sweet garments, bending aside,)
The sea whisper'd me.

ON THE BEACH AT NIGHT

On the beach at night,
Stands a child with her father,
Watching the east, the autumn sky.

Up through the darkness,
While ravening clouds, the burial clouds, in black masses
    spreading,
Lower sullen and fast athwart and down the sky,
Amid a transparent clear belt of ether yet left in the east,
Ascends large and calm the lord-star Jupiter,
And nigh at hand, only a very little above,
Swim the delicate sisters the Pleiades.

From the beach the child holding the hand of her father,
Those burial-clouds that lower victorious soon to devour
    all,
Watching, silently weeps.

Weep not, child,
Weep not, my darling,

With these kisses let me remove your tears,
The ravening clouds shall not long be victorious,
They shall not long possess the sky, they devour the stars
    only in apparition,
Jupiter shall emerge, be patient, watch again another night,
    the Pleiades shall emerge,
They are immortal, all those stars both silvery and golden
    shall shine out again,
The great stars and the little ones shall shine out again,
    they endure,
The vast immortal suns and the long-enduring pensive
    moons shall again shine.

Then dearest child mournest thou only for Jupiter?
Considerest thou alone the burial of the stars?

Something there is,
(With my lips soothing thee, adding I whisper,
I give thee the first suggestion, the problem and
    indirection,)
Something there is more immortal even than the stars,
(Many the burials, many the days and night, passing
    away,)
Something that shall endure longer even than lustrous
    Jupiter,
Longer than sun or any revolving satellite,
Or the radiant sisters the Pleiades.

I Sit and Look Out

I sit and look out upon all the sorrows of the world, and
    upon all oppression and shame,
I hear secret convulsive sobs from young men at anguish
    with themselves, remorseful after deeds done,

I see in low life the mother misused by her children,
    dying, neglected, gaunt, desperate,
I see the wife misused by her husband, I see the
    treacherous seducer of young women,
I mark the ranklings of jealousy and unrequited love
    attempted to be hid, I see these sights on the earth,
I see the workings of battle, pestilence, tyranny, I see
    martyrs and prisoners,
I observe a famine at sea, I observe the sailors casting lots
    who shall be kill'd to preserve the lives of the rest,
I observe the slights and degradations cast by arrogant
    persons upon laborers, the poor, and upon negroes,
    and the like;
All these — all the meanness and agony without end I
    sitting look out upon,
See, hear, and am silent.

THE DALLIANCE OF THE EAGLES

Skirting the river road, (my forenoon walk, my rest,)
Skyward in air a sudden muffled sound, the dalliance of
    the eagles,
The rushing amorous contact high in space together,
The clinching interlocking claws, a living, fierce, gyrating
    wheel,
Four beating wings, two beaks, a swirling mass tight
    grappling,
In tumbling turning clustering loops, straight downward
    falling,
Till o'er the river pois'd, the twain yet one, a moment's
    lull,

A motionless still balance in the air, then parting, talons
    loosing,
Upward again on slow-firm pinions slanting, their separate
    diverse flight,
She hers, he his, pursuing.

THE RUNNER

On a flat road runs the well-train'd runner,
He is lean and sinewy with muscular legs,
He is thinly clothed, he leans forward as he runs,
With lightly closed fists and arms partially rais'd.

HAST NEVER COME TO THEE AN HOUR

Hast never come to thee an hour,
A sudden gleam divine, precipitating, bursting all these
    bubbles, fashions, wealth?
These eager business aims — books, politics, art, amours,
To utter nothingness?

CAVALRY CROSSING A FORD

A line in long array where they wind betwixt green
    islands,
They take a serpentine course, their arms flash in the sun
    — hark to the musical clank,
Behold the silvery river, in it the splashing horses loitering
    stop to drink,
Behold the brown-faced men, each group, each person a
    picture, the negligent rest on the saddles,

Some emerge on the opposite bank, others are just entering
    the ford — while,
Scarlet and blue and snowy white,
The guidon flags flutter gayly in the wind.

COME UP FROM THE FIELDS FATHER

Come up from the fields father, here's a letter from our
    Pete.
And come to the front door mother, here's a letter from
    thy dear son.

Lo, 'tis autumn,
Lo, where the trees, deeper green, yellower and redder,
Cool and sweeten Ohio's villages with leaves fluttering in
    the moderate wind,
Where apples ripe in the orchards hang and grapes on the
    trellis'd vines,
(Smell you the smell of the grapes on the vines?
Smell you the buckwheat where the bees were lately
    buzzing?)

Above all, lo, the sky so calm, so transparent after the rain,
    and with wondrous clouds,
Below too, all calm, all vital and beautiful, and the farm
    prospers well.

Down in the fields all prospers well,
But now from the fields come father, come at the
    daughter's call,
And come to the entry mother, to the front door come
    right away.

Fast as she can she hurries, something ominous, her steps
    trembling,
She does not tarry to smooth her hair nor adjust her cap.

Open the envelope quickly,
O this is not our son's writing, yet his name is sign'd,
O a strange hand writes for our dear son, O stricken
    mother's soul!
All swims before her eyes, flashes with black, she catches
    the main words only,
Sentences broken, *gunshot wound in the breast, cavalry
    skirmish, taken to hospital,*
At present low, but will soon be better.

Ah now the single figure to me,
Amid all teeming and wealthy Ohio with all its cities and
    farms,
Sickly white in the face and dull in the head, very faint,
By the jamb of a door leans.

Grieve not so, dear mother, (the just-grown daughter speaks
    through her sobs,
The little sisters huddle around speechless and dismay'd,)
See, dearest mother, the letter says Pete will soon be better.

Alas poor boy, he will never be better, (nor may-be needs
    to be better, that brave and simple soul,)
While they stand at home at the door he is dead already,
The only son is dead.

But the mother needs to be better,
She with thin form presently drest in black,
By day her meals untouch'd, then at night fitfully sleeping,
    often waking,

In the midnight waking, weeping, longing with one deep
    longing,
O that she might withdraw unnoticed, silent from life
    escape and withdraw,
To follow, to seek, to be with her dear dead son.

A March in the Ranks Hard-Prest, and the Road Unknown

A march in the ranks hard-prest, and the road unknown,
A route through a heavy wood with muffled steps in the
    darkness,
Our army foil'd with loss severe, and the sullen remnant
    retreating,
Till after midnight glimmer upon us the lights of a
    dim-lighted building,
We come to an open space in the woods, and halt by the
    dim-lighted building,
'Tis a large old church at the crossing roads, now an
    impromptu hospital,
Entering but for a minute I see a sight beyond all the
    pictures and poems ever made,
Shadows of deepest, deepest black, just lit by moving
    candles and lamps,
And by one great pitchy torch stationary with wild red
    flame and clouds of smoke,
By these, crowds, groups of forms vaguely I see on the
    floor, some in the pews laid down,
At my feet more distinctly a soldier, a mere lad, in danger
    of bleeding to death, (he is shot in the abdomen,)
I stanch the blood temporarily, (the youngster's face is
    white as a lily,)

Then before I depart I sweep my eyes o'er the scene fain
    to absorb it all,
Faces, varieties, postures beyond description, most in
    obscurity, some of them dead,
Surgeons operating, attendants holding lights, the smell of
    ether, the odor of blood,
The crowd, O the crowd of the bloody forms, the yard
    outside also fill'd,
Some on the bare ground, some on planks or stretchers,
    some in the death-spasm sweating,
An occasional scream or cry, the doctor's shouted orders or
    calls,
The glisten of the little steel instruments catching the glint
    of the torches,
These I resume as I chant, I see again the forms, I smell
    the odor,
Then hear outside the orders given, *Fall in, my men, fall in;*
But first I bend to the dying lad, his eyes open, a
    half-smile gives he me,
Then the eyes close, calmly close, and I speed forth to the
    darkness,
Resuming, marching, ever in darkness marching, on in the
    ranks,
The unknown road still marching.

A Sight in Camp in the Daybreak Gray and Dim

A sight in camp in the daybreak gray and dim,
As from my tent I emerge so early sleepless,
As slow I walk in the cool fresh air the path near by the
    hospital tent,

Three forms I see on stretchers lying, brought out there
    untended lying,
Over each the blanket spread, ample brownish woolen
    blanket,
Gray and heavy blanket, folding, covering all.

Curious I halt and silent stand,
Then with light fingers I from the face of the nearest the
    first just lift the blanket;
Who are you elderly man so gaunt and grim, with
    well-gray'd hair, and flesh all sunken about the eyes?
Who are you my dear comrade?

Then to the second I step — and who are you my child
    and darling?
Who are you sweet boy with cheeks yet blooming?

Then to the third — a face nor child nor old, very calm,
    as of beautiful yellow-white ivory;
Young man I think I know you — I think this face is the
    face of the Christ himself,
Dead and divine and brother of all, and here again he lies.

WHEN LILACS LAST IN THE DOORYARD BLOOM'D

I

When lilacs last in the dooryard bloom'd,
And the great star early droop'd in the western sky in the
    night,
I mourn'd, and yet shall mourn with ever-returning spring.

Ever-returning spring, trinity sure to me you bring,
Lilac blooming perennial and drooping star in the west,
And thought of him I love.

O powerful western fallen star!
O shades of night — O moody, tearful night!
O great star disappear'd — O the black murk that hides
    the star!
O cruel hands that hold me powerless — O helpless soul
    of me!
O harsh surrounding cloud that will not free my soul.

3

In the dooryard fronting an old farm-house near the
    white-wash'd palings,
Stands the lilac-bush tall-growing with heart-shaped leaves
    of rich green,
With many a pointed blossom rising delicate, with the
    perfume strong I love,
With every leaf a miracle — and from this bush in the
    dooryard,
With delicate-color'd blossoms and heart-shaped leaves of
    rich green,
A sprig with its flower I break.

4

In the swamp in secluded recesses,
A shy and hidden bird is warbling a song.

Solitary the thrush,
The hermit withdrawn to himself, avoiding the settlements,
Sings by himself a song.

Song of the bleeding throat,
Death's outlet song of life, (for well dear brother I know,
If thou wast not granted to sing thou would'st surely die.)

Over the breast of the spring, the land, amid cities,
Amid lanes and through old woods, where lately the
    violets peep'd from the ground, spotting the gray
    debris,
Amid the grass in the fields each side of the lanes, passing
    the endless grass,
Passing the yellow-spear'd wheat, every grain from its
    shroud in the dark-brown fields uprisen,
Passing the apple-tree blows of white and pink in the
    orchards,
Carrying a corpse to where it shall rest in the grave,
Night and day journeys a coffin.

Coffin that passes through lanes and streets,
Through day and night with the great cloud darkening the
    land,
With the pomp of the inloop'd flags with the cities draped
    in black,
With the show of the States themselves as of crape-veil'd
    women standing,
With processions long and winding and the flambeaus of
    the night,
With the countless torches lit, with the silent sea of faces
    and the unbared heads,
With the waiting depot, the arriving coffin, and the
    sombre faces,
With dirges through the night, with the thousand voices
    rising strong and solemn,
With all the mournful voices of the dirges pour'd around
    the coffin,

The dim-lit churches and the shuddering organs — where
        amid these you journey,
With the tolling tolling bells' perpetual clang,
Here, coffin that slowly passes,
I give you my sprig of lilac.

7

(Nor for you, for one alone,
Blossoms and branches green to coffins all I bring,
For fresh as the morning, thus would I chant a song for
        you O sane and sacred death.

All over bouquets of roses,
O death, I cover you over with roses and early lilies,
But mostly and now the lilac that blooms the first,
Copious I break, I break the sprigs from the bushes,
With loaded arms I come, pouring for you,
For you and the coffins all of you O death.)

8

O western orb sailing the heaven,
Now I know what you must have meant as a month since
        I walk'd,
As I walk'd in silence the transparent shadowy night,
As I saw you had something to tell as you bent to me
        night after night,
As you droop'd from the sky low down as if to my side,
        (while the other stars all look'd on,)
As we wander'd together the solemn night, (for something
        I know not what kept me from sleep,)

As the night advanced, and I saw on the rim of the west
   how full you were of woe,
As I stood on the rising ground in the breeze in the cool
   transparent night,
As I watch'd where you pass'd and was lost in the
   netherward black of the night,
As my soul in its trouble dissatisfied sank, as where you
   sad orb,
Concluded, dropt in the night, and was gone.

9

Sing on there in the swamp,
O singer bashful and tender, I hear your notes, I hear your
   call,
I hear, I come presently, I understand you,
But a moment I linger, for the lustrous star has detain'd
   me,
The star my departing comrade holds and detains me.

10

O how shall I warble myself for the dead one there I
   loved?
And how shall I deck my song for the large sweet soul
   that has gone?
And what shall my perfume be for the grave of him I
   love?

Sea-winds blown from east and west,
Blown from the Eastern sea and blown from the Western
   sea, till there on the prairies meeting,
These and with these and the breath of my chant,
I'll perfume the grave of him I love.

11

O what shall I hang on the chamber walls?
And what shall the pictures be that I hang on the walls,
To adorn the burial-house of him I love?

Pictures of growing spring and farms and homes,
With the Fourth-month eve at sundown, and the gray
  smoke lucid and bright,
With floods of the yellow gold of the gorgeous, indolent,
  sinking sun, burning, expanding the air,
With the fresh sweet herbage under foot, and the pale
  green leaves of the trees prolific,
In the distance the flowing glaze, the breast of the river,
  with a wind-dapple here and there,
With ranging hills on the banks, with many a line against
  the sky, and shadows,
And the city at hand with dwellings so dense, and stacks
  of chimneys,
And all the scenes of life and the workshops, and the
  workmen homeward returning.

Lo, body and soul — this land,
My own Manhattan with spires, and the sparkling and
  hurrying tides, and the ships,
The varied and ample land, the South and the North in
  the light, Ohio's shores and flashing Missouri,
And ever the far-spreading prairies cover'd with grass and
  corn.

Lo, the most excellent sun so calm and haughty,
The violet and purple morn with just-felt breezes,
The gentle soft-born measureless light,

The miracle spreading bathing all, the fulfill'd noon,
The coming eve delicious, the welcome night and the stars,
Over my cities shining all, enveloping man and land.

13

Sing on, sing on you gray-brown bird,
Sing from the swamps, the recesses, pour your chant from
    the bushes,
Limitless out of the dusk, out of the cedars and pines.

Sing on dearest brother, warble your reedy song,
Loud human song, with voice of uttermost woe.

O liquid and free and tender!
O wild and loose to my soul — O wondrous singer!
You only I hear — yet the star holds me, (but will soon
    depart,)
Yet the lilac with mastering odor holds me.

14

Now while I sat in the day and look'd forth,
In the close of the day with its light and the fields of
    spring, and the farmers preparing their crops,
In the large unconscious scenery of my land with its lakes
    and forests,
In the heavenly aerial beauty, (after the perturb'd winds
    and the storms,)
Under the arching heavens of the afternoon swift passing,
    and the voices of children and women,
The many-moving sea-tides, and I saw the ships how they
    sail'd,
And the summer approaching with richness, and the fields
    all busy with labor,

And the infinite separate houses, how they all went on,
    each with its meals and minutia of daily usages,
And the streets how their throbbings throbb'd, and the
    cities pent — lo, then and there,
Falling upon them all and among them all, enveloping me
    with the rest,
Appear'd the cloud, appear'd the long black trail,
And I knew death, its thought, and the sacred knowledge
    of death.

Then with the knowledge of death as walking one side of
    me,
And the thought of death close-walking the other side of
    me,
And I in the middle as with companions, and as holding
    the hands of companions,
I fled forth to the hiding receiving night that talks not,
Down to the shores of the water, the path by the swamp
    in the dimness,
To the solemn shadowy cedars and ghostly pines so still.

And the singer so shy to the rest receiv'd me,
The gray-brown bird I know receiv'd us comrades three,
And he sang the carol of death, and a verse for him I
    love.

From deep secluded recesses,
From the fragrant cedars and the ghostly pines so still,
Came the carol of the bird.

And the charm of the carol rapt me,
As I held as if by their hands my comrades in the night,
And the voice of my spirit tallied the song of the bird.

Come lovely and soothing death,
Undulate round the world, serenely arriving, arriving,
In the day, in the night, to all, to each,
Sooner or later delicate death.

Prais'd be the fathomless universe,
For life and joy, and for objects and knowledge curious,
And for love, sweet love — but praise! praise! praise!
For the sure-enwinding arms of cool-enfolding death.

Dark mother always gliding near with soft feet,
Have none chanted for thee a chant of fullest welcome?
Then I chant it for thee, I glorify thee above all,
I bring thee a song that when thou must indeed come, come
*   unfalteringly.*

Approach strong deliveress,
When it is so, when thou hast taken them I joyously sing the
*   dead,*
Lost in the loving floating ocean of thee,
Laved in the flood of thy bliss O death.

From me to thee glad serenades,
Dances for thee I propose saluting thee, adornments and
*   feastings for thee,*
And the sights of the open landscape and the high-spread sky
*   are fitting,*
And life and the fields, and the huge and thoughtful night.

The night in silence under many a star,
The ocean shore and the husky whispering wave whose voice I
*   know,*
And the soul turning to thee O vast and well-veil'd death,
And the body gratefully nestling close to thee.

Over the tree-tops I float thee a song,
Over the rising and sinking waves, over the myriad fields and
the prairies wide,
Over the dense-pack'd cities all and the teeming wharves and
ways,
I float this carol with joy, with joy to thee O death.

15

To the tally of my soul,
Loud and strong kept up the gray-brown bird,
With pure deliberate notes spreading filling the night.

Loud in the pines and cedars dim,
Clear in the freshness moist and the swamp-perfume,
And I with my comrades there in the night.

While my sight that was bound in my eyes unclosed,
As to long panoramas of visions.

And I saw askant the armies,
I saw as in noiseless dreams hundreds of battle-flags,
Borne through the smoke of the battles and pierc'd with
missiles I saw them,
And carried hither and yon through the smoke, and torn
and bloody,
And at last but a few shreds left on the staffs, (and all in
silence,)
And the staffs all splinter'd and broken.

I saw battle-corpses, myriads of them,
And the white skeletons of young men, I saw them,
I saw the debris and debris of all the slain soldiers of the
war,
But I saw they were not as was thought,
They themselves were fully at rest, they suffer'd not,

The living remain'd and suffer'd, the mother suffer'd,
And the wife and the child and the musing comrade
     suffer'd,
And the armies that remain'd suffer'd.

16

Passing the visions, passing the night,
Passing, unloosing the hold of my comrades' hands,
Passing the song of the hermit bird and the tallying song
     of my soul,
Victorious song, death's outlet song, yet varying
     ever-altering song,
As low and wailing, yet clear the notes, rising and falling,
     flooding the night,
Sadly sinking and fainting, as warning and warning, and
     yet again bursting with joy,
Covering the earth and filling the spread of the heaven,
As that powerful psalm in the night I heard from recesses,
Passing, I leave thee lilac with heart-shaped leaves,
I leave thee there in the door-yard, blooming, returning
     with spring.

I cease from my song for thee,
From my gaze on thee in the west, fronting the west,
     communing with thee,
O comrade lustrous with silver face in the night.

Yet each to keep and all, retrievements out of the night,
The song, the wondrous chant of the gray-brown bird,
And the tallying chant, the echo arous'd in my soul,
With the lustrous and drooping star with the countenance
     full of woe,
With the holders holding my hand nearing the call of the
     bird,

Comrades mine and I in the midst, and their memory ever
    to keep, for the dead I loved so well,
For the sweetest, wisest soul of all my days and lands —
    and this for his dear sake,
Lilac and star and bird twined with the chant of my soul,
There in the fragrant pines and the cedars dusk and dim.

O CAPTAIN! MY CAPTAIN!

O Captain! my Captain! our fearful trip is done,
The ship has weather'd every rack, the prize we sought is
    won,
The port is near, the bells I hear, the people all exulting,
While follow eyes the steady keel, the vessel grim and
    daring;
            But O heart! heart! heart!
                O the bleeding drops of red,
                    Where on the deck my Captain lies,
                        Fallen cold and dead.

O Captain! my Captain! rise up and hear the bells;
Rise up — for you the flag is flung — for you the bugle
    trills,
For you bouquets and ribbon'd wreaths — for you the
    shores a-crowding,
For you they call, the swaying mass, their eager faces
    turning;
            Here Captain! dear father!
                This arm beneath your head!
                    It is some dream that on the deck,
                        You've fallen cold and dead.

My Captain does not answer, his lips are pale and still,
My father does not feel my arm, he has no pulse nor will,

The ship is anchor'd safe and sound, its voyage closed and
    done,
From fearful trip the victor ship comes in with object won;
        Exult O shores, and ring O bells!
        But I with mournful tread,
           Walk the deck my Captain lies,
           Fallen cold and dead.

HUSH'D BE THE CAMPS TO-DAY

(May 4, 1865.)

Hush'd be the camps to-day,
And soldiers let us drape our war-worn weapons,
And each with musing soul retire to celebrate,
Our dear commander's death.

No more for him life's stormy conflicts,
Nor victory, nor defeat — no more time's dark events,
Charging like ceaseless clouds across the sky.

But sing poet in our name,
Sing of the love we bore him — because you, dweller in
    camps, know it truly.

As they invault the coffin there,
Sing — as they close the doors of earth upon him — one
    verse,
For the heavy hearts of soldiers.

THERE WAS A CHILD WENT FORTH

There was a child went forth every day,
And the first object he look'd upon, that object he became,

And that object became part of him for the day or a
　　certain part of the day,
Or for many years or stretching cycles of years.

The early lilacs became part of this child,
And grass and white and red morning-glories, and white
　　and red clover, and the song of the phœbe-bird,
And the Third-month lambs and the sow's pink-faint litter,
　　and the mare's foal and the cow's calf,
And the noisy brood of the barnyard or by the mire of
　　the pond-side,
And the fish suspending themselves so curiously below
　　there, and the beautiful curious liquid,
And the water-plants with their graceful flat heads, all
　　became part of him.

The field-sprouts of Fourth-month and Fifth-month
　　became part of him,
Winter-grain sprouts and those of the light-yellow corn,
　　and the esculent roots of the garden,
And the apple-trees cover'd with blossoms and the fruit
　　afterward, and wood-berries, and the commonest
　　weeds by the road,
And the old drunkard staggering home from the outhouse
　　of the tavern whence he had lately risen,
And the schoolmistress that pass'd on her way to the
　　school,
And the friendly boys that pass'd, and the quarrelsome
　　boys,
And the tidy and fresh-cheek'd girls, and the barefoot
　　negro boy and girl,
And all the changes of city and country wherever he went.

His own parents, he that had father'd him and she that had
  conceiv'd him in her womb and birth'd him,
They gave this child more of themselves than that,
They gave him afterward every day, they became part of
  him.

The mother at home quietly placing the dishes on the
  supper-table,
The mother with mild words, clean her cap and gown, a
  wholesome odor falling off her person and clothes as
  she walks by,
The father, strong, self-sufficient, manly, mean, anger'd,
  unjust,
The blow, the quick loud word, the tight bargain, the
  crafty lure,
The family usages, the language, the company, the
  furniture, the yearning and swelling heart,
Affection that will not be gainsay'd, the sense of what is
  real, the thought if after all it should prove unreal,
The doubts of day-time and the doubts of night-time, the
  curious whether and how,
Whether that which appears so is so, or is it all flashes and
  specks?
Men and women crowding fast in the streets, if they are
  not flashes and specks what are they?
The streets themselves and the façades of houses, and goods
  in the windows,
Vehicles, teams, the heavy-plank'd wharves, the huge
  crossing at the ferries,
The village on the highland seen from afar at sunset, the
  river between,
Shadows, aureola and mist, the light falling on roofs and
  gables of white or brown two miles off,

The schooner near by sleepily dropping down the tide, the
    little boat slack-tow'd astern,
The hurrying tumbling waves, quick-broken crests,
    slapping,
The strata of color'd clouds, the long bar of maroon-tint
    away solitary by itself, the spread of purity it lies
    motionless in,
The horizon's edge, the flying sea-crow, the fragrance of
    salt marsh and shore mud,
These became part of that child who went forth every day,
    and who now goes, and will always go forth every
    day.

MIRACLES

Why, who makes much of a miracle?
As to me I know of nothing else but miracles,
Whether I walk the streets of Manhattan,
Or dart my sight over the roofs of houses toward the sky,
Or wade with naked feet along the beach just in the edge
    of the water,
Or stand under trees in the woods,
Or talk by day with any one I love, or sleep in the bed at
    night with any one I love,
Or sit at table at dinner with the rest,
Or look at strangers opposite me riding in the car,
Or watch honey-bees busy around the hive of a summer
    forenoon,
Or animals feeding in the fields,
Or birds, or the wonderfulness of insects in the air,
Or the wonderfulness of the sundown, or of stars shining
    so quiet and bright,

Or the exquisite delicate thin curve of the new moon in
    spring;
These with the rest, one and all, are to me miracles,
The whole referring, yet each distinct and in its place.

To me every hour of the light and dark is a miracle,
Every cubic inch of space is a miracle,
Every square yard of the surface of the earth is spread
    with the same,
Every foot of the interior swarms with the same.

To me the sea is a continual miracle,
The fishes that swim — the rocks — the motion of the
    waves — the ships with men in them,
What stranger miracles are there?

SPARKLES FROM THE WHEEL

Where the city's ceaseless crowd moves on the livelong
    day,
Withdrawn I join a group of children watching, I pause
    aside with them.

By the curb toward the edge of the flagging,
A knife-grinder works at his wheel sharpening a great
    knife,
Bending over he carefully holds it to the stone, by foot
    and knee,
With measur'd tread he turns rapidly, as he presses with
    light but firm hand,
Forth issue then in copious golden jets,
Sparkles from the wheel.

The scene and all its belongings, how they seize and affect
    me,

The sad sharp-chinn'd old man with worn clothes and
    broad shoulder-band of leather,
Myself effusing and fluid, a phantom curiously floating,
    now here absorb'd and arrested,
The group, (an unminded point set in a vast surrounding,)
The attentive, quiet children, the loud, proud, restive base
    of the streets,
The low hoarse purr of the whirling stone, the
    light-press'd blade,
Diffusing, dropping, sideways-darting, in tiny showers of
    gold,
Sparkles from the wheel.

THE TORCH

On my Northwest coast in the midst of the night a
    fishermen's group stands watching,
Out on the lake that expands before them, others are
    spearing salmon,
The canoe, a dim shadowy thing, moves across the black
    water,
Bearing a torch ablaze at the prow.

AS IF A PHANTOM CARESS'D ME

As if a phantom caress'd me,
I thought I was not alone walking here by the shore;
But the one I thought was with me as now I walk by the
    shore, the one I loved that caress'd me,
As I lean and look through the glimmering light, that one
    has utterly disappear'd,
And those appear that are hateful to me and mock me.

A NOISELESS PATIENT SPIDER

A noiseless patient spider,
I mark'd where on a little promontory it stood isolated,
Mark'd how to explore the vacant vast surrounding,
It launch'd forth filament, filament, filament, out of itself,
Ever unreeling them, ever tirelessly speeding them.

And you O my soul where you stand,
Surrounded, detached, in measureless oceans of space,
Ceaselessly musing, venturing, throwing, seeking the
    spheres to connect them,
Till the bridge you will need be form'd, till the ductile
    anchor hold,
Till the gossamer thread you fling catch somewhere, O my
    soul.

EXCELSIOR

Who has gone farthest? for I would go farther,
And who has been just? for I would be the most just
    person of the earth,
And who most cautious? for I would be more cautious,
And who has been happiest? O I think it is I — I think no
    one was ever happier than I,
And who has lavish'd all? for I lavish constantly the best I
    have,
And who proudest? for I think I have reason to be the
    proudest son alive — for I am the son of the brawny
    and tall-topt city,
And who has been bold and true? for I would be the
    boldest and truest being of the universe,

And who benevolent? for I would show more benevolence
   than all the rest,
And who has receiv'd the love of the most friends? for I
   know what it is to receive the passionate love of
   many friends,
And who possesses a perfect and enamour'd body? for I do
   not believe any one possesses a more perfect or
   enamour'd body than mine,
And who thinks the amplest thoughts? for I would
   surround those thoughts,
And who has made hymns fit for the earth? for I am mad
   with devouring ecstasy to make joyous hymns for the
   whole earth.

A Clear Midnight

This is thy hour O Soul, thy free flight into the wordless,
Away from books, away from art, the day erased, the
   lesson done,
Thee fully forth emerging, silent, gazing, pondering the
   themes thou lovest best,
Night, sleep, death and the stars.

Thanks in Old Age

Thanks in old age — thanks ere I go,
For health, the midday sun, the impalpable air — for life,
   mere life,
For precious ever-lingering memories, (of you my mother
   dear — you, father — you, brothers, sisters, friends,)
For all my days — not those of peace alone — the days of
   war the same,

For gentle words, caresses, gifts from foreign lands,
For shelter, wine and meat — for sweet appreciation,
(You distant, dim unknown — or young or old —
    countless, unspecified, readers belov'd,
We never met, and ne'er shall meet — and yet our souls
    embrace, long, close and long;)
For beings, groups, love, deeds, words, books — for colors,
    forms,
For all the brave strong men — devoted, hardy men —
    who've forward sprung in freedom's help, all years,
    all lands,
For braver, stronger, more devoted men — (a special laurel
    ere I go, to life's war's chosen ones,
The cannoneers of song and thought — the great artillerists
    — the foremost leaders, captains of the soul:)
As soldier from an ended war return'd — As traveler out
    of myriads, to the long procession retrospective,
Thanks — joyful thanks! — a soldier's, traveler's thanks.

GOOD-BYE MY FANCY!

Good-bye my Fancy!
Farewell dear mate, dear love!
I'm going away, I know not where,
Or to what fortune, or whether I may ever see you again,
So Good-bye my Fancy.

Now for my last — let me look back a moment;
The slower fainter ticking of the clock is in me,
Exit, nightfall, and soon the heart-thud stopping.

Long have we lived, joy'd, caress'd together;
Delightful! — now separation — Good-bye my Fancy.

Yet let me not be too hasty,
Long indeed have we lived, slept, filter'd, become really
  blended into one;
Then if we die we die together, (yes, we'll remain one,)
If we go anywhere we'll go together to meet what
  happens,
May-be we'll be better off and blither, and learn
  something.
May-be it is yourself now really ushering me to the true
  songs, (who knows?)
May-be it is you the mortal knob really undoing, turning
  — so now finally,
Good-bye — and hail! my Fancy.

Unlike Whitman, who rarely hung his hat in the same place for long, Emily Elizabeth Dickinson spent nearly her entire life in the Amherst, Massachusetts, house where she was born in 1830 and where, fifty-six years later, she died. If our image of Whitman is of a gregarious fellow sauntering down a crowded avenue, we tend, somewhat condescendingly, to picture the virginal "nun of Amherst," dressed all in white, slipping upstairs to the solitude of the quiet bedroom where she wrote the poems that made her famous, or perhaps in the kitchen, preparing treats for the neighborhood children or baking the rye bread that won second prize in a country fair. In any case, except for brief periods of study at Mount Holyoke College (then called Mount Holyoke Female Seminary), several visits to Boston, and a trip, when she was twenty-three, to Washington and

Philadelphia, she rarely ventured past the borders of her own yard.

Though such an utter rejection of mobility may seem eccentric, even perverse, there is no reason to assume that the life of this sequestered woman was lacking in satisfactions or that she had any less intellectual curiosity than those of us accumulating frequent-flyer miles. With so finely tuned an imagination as hers, an up-to-date passport would have been redundant:

> I never saw a Moor —
> I never saw the Sea —
> Yet know I how the Heather looks
> And what a Billow be.

Anything but a total recluse, she enjoyed the society of her prosperous lawyer father (who was treasurer of Amherst College), an unmarried sister, who lived at home, and an older brother, who lived next door with his wife. She also relished the unthreatening intimacy of long-distance relationships, writing upwards of ten thousand letters, characterized by the pungent observations, odd imagery, and peculiar punctuation that distinguish her poems. They also reveal her pointed wit. When a friend sent her sister and her a joint letter she protested: "A mutual plum is not a plum. I was too respectful to take the pulp and do not like the stone." She read the Springfield (Mass.) *Republican* every day to keep up with what was happening in the larger world and enjoyed the stimulating companionship of books, those "strongest friends of the soul." Her poems, not surprisingly, are seasoned with oblique allusions to other writers. She loved the Bible, the Brontës, George Eliot, Keats, Emerson (her intellectual "validator"), Sir Thomas Browne, and especially Shakespeare—"Why," she asked, "is any other book needed?" She never read Whitman, having been told that he was "disgraceful."

Dickinson was the sort of audience every writer dreams of. "If I read a book," she observed, "and it makes my body so cold no fire can ever warm me I know *that* is poetry. If I feel physically as if the top of my head were taken off, I know *that* is poetry. These are the way I know it. Is there any other way?" It is clear that her writing also provided intellectual and sensual excitement at a high pitch. When we realize that she wrote scores of poems every year, any thought that her life was without drama quickly disappears. It is difficult, in fact, to imagine a life lived more passionately, even if the passion falls outside what we think of as erotic or romantic love. Certain biographers, feeling compelled to explain away the "retreat" of this strange and original genius, have suggested that she suffered the heartbreak of a frustrated affair, but though some drafts of letters are addressed to a man she called Master, no conclusive evidence of an affair has presented itself. In her late forties she enjoyed a warm relationship with a widowed judge, a close friend of her father's, but the reciprocated love did not lead to marriage. Every now and then, Emerson said, an individual exquisitely made can live alone. For a poet, as Marianne Moore put it, "there is society in solitude." "I find ecstasy in living," Dickinson wrote a friend. "The mere sense of living is joy enough."

She stopped going to church at an early age, unable to accept the idea of Original Sin, and instead sought spiritual solace away from the family pew.

> Some keep the Sabbath going to Church —
> I keep it, staying at Home —
> With a Bobolink for a Chorister —
> And an Orchard, for a Dome —

The hymns she had heard all her life remained with her, however, providing the form and meter for her poems, some of which employ biblical imagery to stress her estrangement from orthodox theological views as she grapples with immensities and terrors.

Taking liberties with the regular hymnbook meter through intentionally jarring rhythmical variations, she also employed off rhymes, or near rhymes, to ensure that the quatrains, couched in "the language of surprise," were neither conventional nor predictable.

> A Man may make a Remark —
> In itself — a quiet thing
> That may furnish the Fuse unto a Spark
> In dormant nature — lain
>
> Let us deport — with skill —
> Let us discourse — with care —
> Powder exists in Charcoal —
> Before it exists in Fire.

Rarely containing so much as an unnecessary syllable, the poems are almost all characterized by an epigrammatic precision. Only a handful were published during her lifetime (five of them in the *Republican*), and as a result she had no reputation at all. It was not until several years after her death, when a volume of 116 poems appeared, that she began to acquire an audience: that small collection went through eleven editions in just two years.

"Tell all the Truth," she said, "but tell it slant." A reader soon learns the pleasures of collaboration, filling in the missing keys she has deliberately left out. Her hundreds of enigmatic lyrics, alternately playful and darkly cryptic, tell the truth in her original way about the things that preoccupied her thoughts — domestic details, pain, joy, beauty, the evanescent drama of nature, death.

> The Bustle in a House
> The Morning after Death
> Is solemnest of industries
> Enacted upon Earth —
>
> The Sweeping up the Heart
> And putting Love away
> We shall not want to use again
> Until Eternity.

What mainly held her attention, year after year, was the mysterious power of words. "We used to think," she wrote a friend, "that words were cheap & weak. Now I don't know of anything so mighty. There are [some] to which I lift my hat when I see them sitting princelike among their peers on the page. Sometimes I write one, and look at his outlines till he glows as no sapphire."

"Hope" is the thing with feathers —
That perches in the soul —
And sings the tune without the words —
And never stops — at all —

And sweetest — in the Gale — is heard —
And sore must be the storm —
That could abash the little Bird
That kept so many warm —

I've heard it in the chillest land —
And on the strangest Sea —
Yet, never, in Extremity,
It asked a crumb — of Me.

The numbers on the poems in this section are taken from a one-volume edition, superbly edited by Thomas H. Johnson, in which the 1,775 poems are printed in probable chronological order: *The Complete Poems of Emily Dickinson* (Little, Brown, 1960). There is an excellent biography in paperback: Richard B. Sewall, *The Life of Emily Dickinson* (Farrar, Straus & Giroux, 1974). For very detailed information about the poet and her Amherst world, see Jay Leyda, *The Years and Hours of Emily Dickinson,* two volumes (Yale University Press, 1960). For criticism, see Christopher Benfey, *Emily Dickinson: The Lives of a Poet* (George Braziller, 1986); Charles R. Anderson, *Emily Dickinson's Poetry: Stairway of Surprise* (Holt, Rinehart & Winston, 1960); and Cynthia Griffin Wolff, *Emily Dickinson* (Alfred A. Knopf, 1986).

12

The morns are meeker than they were —
The nuts are getting brown —
The berry's cheek is plumper —
The Rose is out of town.

The Maple wears a gayer scarf —
The field a scarlet gown —

Lest I should be old fashioned
I'll put a trinket on.

47

Heart! We will forget him!
You and I — tonight!
You may forget the warmth he gave —
I will forget the light!

When you have done, pray tell me
That I may straight begin!
Haste! lest while you're lagging
I remember him!

67

Success is counted sweetest
By those who ne'er succeed.
To comprehend a nectar
Requires sorest need.

Not one of all the purple Host
Who took the Flag today
Can tell the definition
So clear of Victory

As he defeated — dying —
On whose forbidden ear
The distant strains of triumph
Burst agonized and clear!

77

I never hear the word "escape"
Without a quicker blood,
A sudden expectation,
A flying attitude!

I never hear of prisons broad
By soldiers battered down,
But I tug childish at my bars
Only to fail again!

108

Surgeons must be very careful
When they take the knife!
Underneath their fine incisions
Stirs the Culprit — *Life*!

193

I shall know why — when Time is over —
And I have ceased to wonder why —
Christ will explain each separate anguish
In the fair schoolroom of the sky —

He will tell me what "Peter" promised —
And I — for wonder at his woe —
I shall forget the drop of Anguish
That scalds me now — that scalds me now!

254

"Hope" is the thing with feathers —
That perches in the soul —
And sings the tune without the words —
And never stops — at all —

And sweetest — in the Gale — is heard —
And sore must be the storm —
That could abash the little Bird
That kept so many warm —

I've heard it in the chillest land —
And on the strangest Sea —
Yet, never, in Extremity,
It asked a crumb — of Me.

258

There's a certain Slant of light,
Winter Afternoons —
That oppresses, like the Heft
Of Cathedral Tunes —

Heavenly Hurt, it gives us —
We can find no scar,
But internal difference,
Where the Meanings, are —

None may teach it — Any —
'Tis the Seal Despair —
An imperial affliction
Sent us of the Air —

When it comes, the Landscape listens —
Shadows — hold their breath —
When it goes, 'tis like the Distance
On the look of Death —

288

I'm Nobody! Who are you?
Are you — Nobody — Too?
Then there's a pair of us!
Don't tell! they'd advertise — you know!

How dreary — to be — Somebody!
How public — like a Frog —
To tell one's name — the livelong June —
To an admiring Bog!

303

The Soul selects her own Society —
Then — shuts the Door —
To her divine Majority —
Present no more —

Unmoved — she notes the Chariots — pausing —
At her low Gate —
Unmoved — an Emperor be kneeling
Upon her Mat —

I've known her — from an ample nation —
Choose One —
Then — close the Valves of her attention —
Like Stone —

328

A Bird came down the Walk —
He did not know I saw —
He bit an Angleworm in halves
And ate the fellow, raw,

And then he drank a Dew
From a convenient Grass —
And then hopped sidewise to the Wall
To let a Beetle pass —

He glanced with rapid eyes
That hurried all around —
They looked like frightened Beads, I thought —
He stirred his Velvet Head

Like one in danger, Cautious,
I offered him a Crumb
And he unrolled his feathers
And rowed him softer home —

Than Oars divide the Ocean,
Too silver for a seam —
Or Butterflies, off Banks of Noon
Leap, plashless as they swim.

341

After great pain, a formal feeling comes —
The Nerves sit ceremonious, like Tombs —
The stiff Heart questions was it He, that bore,
And Yesterday, or Centuries before?

The Feet, mechanical, go round —
Of Ground, or Air, or Ought —
A Wooden way
Regardless grown,
A Quartz contentment, like a stone —

This is the Hour of Lead —
Remembered, if outlived,
As Freezing persons, recollect the Snow —
First — Chill — then Stupor — then the
    letting go —

389

There's been a Death, in the Opposite House,
As lately as Today —
I know it, by the numb look
Such Houses have — alway —

The Neighbors rustle in and out —
The Doctor — drives away —
A Window opens like a Pod —
Abrupt — mechanically —

Somebody flings a Mattress out —
The Children hurry by —
They wonder if it died — on that —
I used to — when a Boy —

The Minister — goes stiffly in —
As if the House were His —

And He owned all the Mourners — now —
And little Boys — besides —

And then the Milliner — and the Man
Of the Appalling Trade —
To take the measure of the House —
There'll be that Dark Parade —

Of Tassels — and of Coaches — soon —
It's easy as a Sign —
The Intuition of the News —
In just a Country Town —

405

It might be lonelier
Without the Loneliness —
I'm so accustomed to my Fate —
Perhaps the Other — Peace —

Would interrupt the Dark —
And crowd the little Room —
Too scant — by Cubits — to contain
The Sacrament — of Him —

I am not used to Hope —
It might intrude upon —
Its sweet parade — blaspheme the place —
Ordained to Suffering —

It might be easier
To fail — with Land in Sight —
Than gain — My Blue Peninsula —
To perish — of Delight —

419

We grow accustomed to the Dark —
When Light is put away —
As when the Neighbor holds the Lamp
To witness her Goodbye —

A Moment — We uncertain step
For newness of the night —
Then — fit our Vision to the Dark —
And meet the Road — erect —

And so of larger — Darknesses —
Those Evenings of the Brain —
When not a Moon disclose a sign —
Or Star — come out — within —

The Bravest — grope a little —
And sometimes hit a Tree
Directly in the Forehead —
But as they learn to see —

Either the Darkness alters —
Or something in the sight
Adjusts itself to Midnight —
And Life steps almost straight.

435

Much Madness is divinest Sense —
To a discerning Eye —
Much Sense — the starkest Madness —
'Tis the Majority

In this, as All, prevail —
Assent — and you are sane —
Demur — you're straightway dangerous —
And handled with a Chain —

441

This is my letter to the World
That never wrote to Me —
The simple News that Nature told —
With tender Majesty

Her Message is committed
To Hands I cannot see —
For love of Her — Sweet — countrymen —
Judge tenderly — of Me

449

I died for Beauty — but was scarce
Adjusted in the Tomb
When One who died for Truth, was lain
In an adjoining Room —

He questioned softly "Why I failed"?
"For Beauty", I replied —
"And I — for Truth — Themself are One —
We Brethren, are", He said —

And so, as Kinsmen, met a Night —
We talked between the Rooms —
Until the Moss had reached our lips —
And covered up — our names —

465

I heard a Fly buzz — when I died —
The Stillness in the Room
Was like the Stillness in the Air —
Between the Heaves of Storm —

The Eyes around — had wrung them dry —
And Breaths were gathering firm
For that last Onset — when the King
Be witnessed — in the Room —

I willed my Keepsakes — Signed away
What portion of me be
Assignable — and then it was
There interposed a Fly —

With Blue — uncertain stumbling Buzz —
Between the light — and me —
And then the Windows failed — and then
I could not see to see —

472

Except the Heaven had come so near —
So seemed to choose My Door —
The Distance would not haunt me so —
I had not hoped — before —

But just to hear the Grace depart —
I never thought to see —
Afflicts me with a Double loss —
'Tis lost — And lost to me —

507

She sights a Bird — she chuckles —
She flattens — then she crawls —
She runs without the look of feet —
Her eyes increase to Balls —

Her Jaws stir — twitching — hungry —
Her Teeth can hardly stand —
She leaps, but Robin leaped the first —
Ah, Pussy, of the Sand,

The Hopes so juicy ripening —
You almost bathed your Tongue —
When Bliss disclosed a hundred Toes —
And fled with every one —

510

It was not Death, for I stood up,
And all the Dead, lie down —
It was not Night, for all the Bells
Put out their Tongues, for Noon.

It was not Frost, for on my Flesh
I felt Siroccos — crawl —
Nor Fire — for just my Marble feet
Could keep a Chancel, cool —

And yet, it tasted, like them all,
The Figures I have seen
Set orderly, for Burial,
Reminded me, of mine —

As if my life were shaven,
And fitted to a frame,
And could not breathe without a key,
And 'twas like Midnight, some —

When everything that ticked — has stopped —
And Space stares all around —
Or Grisly frosts — first Autumn morns,
Repeal the Beating Ground —

But, most, like Chaos — Stopless — cool —
Without a Chance, or Spar —
Or even a Report of Land —
To justify — Despair.

529

I'm sorry for the Dead — Today —
It's such congenial times
Old Neighbors have at fences —
It's time o' year for Hay.

And Broad — Sunburned Acquaintance
Discourse between the Toil —
And laugh, a homely species
That makes the Fences smile —

It seems so straight to lie away
From all the noise of Fields —
The Busy Carts — the fragrant Cocks —
The Mower's Metre — Steals

A Trouble lest they're homesick —
Those Farmers — and their Wives —
Set separate from the Farming —
And all the Neighbors' lives —

A Wonder if the Sepulchre
Don't feel a lonesome way —
When Men — and Boys — and Carts — and June,
Go down the Fields to "Hay" —

540

I took my Power in my Hand —
And went against the World —
'Twas not so much as David — had —
But I — was twice as bold —

I aimed my Pebble — but Myself
Was all the one that fell —
Was it Goliah — was too large —
Or was myself — too small?

556

The Brain, within its Groove
Runs evenly — and true —
But let a Splinter swerve —
'Twere easier for You —

To put a Current back —
When Floods have slit the Hills —
And scooped a Turnpike for Themselves —
And trodden out the Mills —

579

I had been hungry, all the Years —
My Noon had Come — to dine —
I trembling drew the Table near —
And touched the Curious Wine —

'Twas this on Tables I had seen —
When turning, hungry, Home
I looked in Windows, for the Wealth
I could not hope — for Mine —

I did not know the ample Bread —
'Twas so unlike the Crumb
The Birds and I, had often shared
In Nature's — Dining Room —

The Plenty hurt me — 'twas so new —
Myself felt ill — and odd —
As Berry — of a Mountain Bush —
Transplanted — to the Road —

Nor was I hungry — so I found
That Hunger — was a way
Of Persons outside Windows —
The Entering — takes away —

584

It ceased to hurt me, though so slow
I could not feel the Anguish go —
But only knew by looking back —
That something — had benumbed the Track —

Nor when it altered, I could say,
For I had worn it, every day,
As constant as the Childish frock —
I hung upon the Peg, at night.

But not the Grief — that nestled close
As needles — ladies softly press
To Cushions Cheeks —
To keep their place —

Nor what consoled it, I could trace —
Except, whereas 'twas Wilderness —
It's better — almost Peace —

609

I Years had been from Home
And now before the Door
I dared not enter, lest a Face
I never saw before

Stare stolid into mine
And ask my Business there —
"My Business but a Life I left
Was such remaining there?"

I leaned upon the Awe —
I lingered with Before —
The Second like an Ocean rolled
And broke against my ear —

I laughed a crumbling Laugh
That I could fear a Door
Who Consternation compassed
And never winced before.

I fitted to the Latch
My Hand, with trembling care
Lest back the awful Door should spring
And leave me in the Floor —

Then moved my Fingers off
As cautiously as Glass
And held my ears, and like a Thief
Fled gasping from the House —

661

Could I but ride indefinite
As doth the Meadow Bee
And visit only where I liked
And No one visit me

And flirt all Day with Buttercups
And marry whom I may
And dwell a little everywhere
Or better, run away

With no Police to follow
Or chase Him if He do

Till He should jump Peninsulas
To get away from me —

I said "But just to be a Bee"
Upon a Raft of Air
And row in Nowhere all Day long
And anchor "off the Bar"

What Liberty! So Captives deem
Who tight in Dungeons are.

712

Because I could not stop for Death —
He kindly stopped for me —
The Carriage held but just Ourselves —
And Immortality.

We slowly drove — He knew no haste
And I had put away
My labor and my leisure too,
For His Civility —

We passed the School, where Children strove
At Recess — in the Ring —
We passed the Fields of Gazing Grain —
We passed the Setting Sun —

Or rather — He passed Us —
The Dews drew quivering and chill —
For only Gossamer, my Gown —
My Tippet — only Tulle —

We paused before a House that seemed
A Swelling of the Ground —
The Roof was scarcely visible —
The Cornice — in the Ground —

Since then — 'tis Centuries — and yet
Feels shorter than the Day
I first surmised the Horses' Heads
Were toward Eternity —

739

I many times thought Peace had come
When Peace was far away —
As Wrecked Men — deem they sight the Land —
At Centre of the Sea —

And struggle slacker — but to prove
As hopelessly as I —
How many the fictitious Shores —
Before the Harbor be —

744

Remorse — is Memory — awake —
Her Parties all astir —
A Presence of Departed Acts —
At window — and at Door —

Its Past — set down before the Soul
And lighted with a Match —
Perusal — to facilitate —
And help Belief to stretch —

Remorse is cureless — the Disease
Not even God — can heal —
For 'tis His institution — and
The Adequate of Hell —

754

My Life had stood — a Loaded Gun —
In Corners — till a Day
The Owner passed — identified —
And carried Me away —

And now We roam in Sovereign Woods —
And now We hunt the Doe —
And every time I speak for Him —
The Mountains straight reply —

And do I smile, such cordial light
Upon the Valley glow —
It is as a Vesuvian face
Had let its pleasure through —

And when at Night — Our good Day done —
I guard My Master's Head —
'Tis better than the Eider-Duck's
Deep Pillow — to have shared —

To foe of His — I'm deadly foe —
None stir the second time —
On whom I lay a Yellow Eye —
Or an emphatic Thumb —

Though I than He — may longer live
He longer must — than I —
For I have but the power to kill,
Without — the power to die —

875

I stepped from Plank to Plank
A slow and cautious way
The Stars about my Head I felt
About my Feet the Sea.

I knew not but the next
Would be my final inch —
This gave me that precarious Gait
Some call Experience.

EMILY DICKINSON   95

916

His Feet are shod with Gauze —
His Helmet, is of Gold,
His Breast, a Single Onyx
With Chrysophrase, inlaid.

His Labor is a Chant —
His Idleness — a Tune —
Oh, for a Bee's experience
Of Clovers, and of Noon!

952

A Man may make a Remark —
In itself — a quiet thing
That may furnish the Fuse unto a Spark
In dormant nature — lain —

Let us deport — with skill —
Let us discourse — with care —
Powder exists in Charcoal —
Before it exists in Fire.

974

The Soul's distinct connection
With immortality
Is best disclosed by Danger
Or quick Calamity —

As Lightning on a Landscape
Exhibits Sheets of Place —
Not yet suspected — but for Flash —
And Click — and Suddenness.

986

A narrow Fellow in the Grass
Occasionally rides —
You may have met Him — did you not
His notice sudden is —

The Grass divides as with a Comb —
A spotted shaft is seen —
And then it closes at your feet
And opens further on —

He likes a Boggy Acre
A Floor too cool for Corn —
Yet when a Boy, and Barefoot —
I more than once at Noon
Have passed, I thought, a Whip lash
Unbraiding in the Sun
When stooping to secure it
It wrinkled, and was gone —

Several of Nature's People
I know, and they know me —
I feel for them a transport
Of cordiality —

But never met this Fellow
Attended, or alone
Without a tighter breathing
And Zero at the Bone —

1035

Bee! I'm expecting you!
Was saying Yesterday
To Somebody you know
That you were due —

The Frogs got Home last Week —
Are settled, and at work —
Birds, mostly back —
The Clover warm and thick —

You'll get my Letter by
The seventeenth; Reply
Or better, be with me —
Yours, Fly.

1052

I never saw a Moor —
I never saw the Sea —
Yet know I how the Heather looks
And what a Billow be.

I never spoke with God
Nor visited in Heaven —
Yet certain am I of the spot
As if the Checks were given —

1078

The Bustle in a House
The Morning after Death
Is solemnest of industries
Enacted upon Earth —

The Sweeping up the Heart
And putting Love away
We shall not want to use again
Until Eternity.

1096

These Strangers, in a foreign World,
Protection asked of me —
Befriend them, lest Yourself in Heaven
Be found a Refugee —

1198

A soft Sea washed around the House
A Sea of Summer Air
And rose and fell the magic Planks
That sailed without a care —
For Captain was the Butterfly
For Helmsman was the Bee
And an entire universe
For the delighted crew.

1212

A word is dead
When it is said,
Some say.
I say it just
Begins to live
That day.

1222

The Riddle we can guess
We speedily despise —
Not anything is stale so long
As Yesterday's surprise —

1256

Not any higher stands the Grave
For Heroes than for Men —
Not any nearer for the Child
Than numb Three Score and Ten —

This latest Leisure equal lulls
The Beggar and his Queen
Propitiate this Democrat
A Summer's Afternoon —

1263

There is no Frigate like a Book
To take us Lands away
Nor any Coursers like a Page

Of prancing Poetry —
This Traverse may the poorest take
Without oppress of Toll —
How frugal is the Chariot
That bears the Human soul.

1287

In this short Life
That only lasts an hour
How much — how little — is
Within our power

1406

No Passenger was known to flee —
That lodged a night in memory —
That wily — subterranean Inn
Contrives that none go out again —

1448

How soft a Caterpillar steps —
I find one on my Hand
From such a velvet world it comes
Such plushes at command
Its soundless travels just arrest
My slow — terrestrial eye
Intent upon its own career
What use has it for me —

1455

Opinion is a flitting thing,
But Truth, outlasts the Sun —
If then we cannot own them both —
Possess the oldest one —

1465

Before you thought of Spring
Except as a Surmise
You see — God bless his suddenness —
A Fellow in the Skies
Of independent Hues
A little weather worn
Inspiriting habiliments
Of Indigo and Brown —
With specimens of Song
As if for you to choose —
Discretion in the interval
With gay delays he goes
To some superior Tree
Without a single Leaf
And shouts for joy to Nobody
But his seraphic self —

1544

Who has not found the Heaven — below —
Will fail of it above —
For Angels rent the House next ours,
Wherever we remove —

1593

There came a Wind like a Bugle —
It quivered through the Grass
And a Green Chill upon the Heat
So ominous did pass
We barred the Windows and the Doors
As from an Emerald Ghost —
The Doom's electric Moccasin
That very instant passed —
On a strange Mob of panting Trees
And Fences fled away
And Rivers where the Houses ran
Those looked that lived — that Day —
The Bell within the steeple wild
The flying tidings told —
How much can come
And much can go,
And yet abide the World!

1624

Apparently with no surprise
To any happy Flower
The Frost beheads it at its play —
In accidental power —
The blonde Assassin passes on —
The Sun proceeds unmoved
To measure off another Day
For an Approving God.

1627

The Pedigree of Honey
Does not concern the Bee —
A Clover, any time, to him,
Is Aristocracy —

1644

Some one prepared this mighty show
To which without a Ticket go
The nations and the Days —

Displayed before the simplest Door
That all may witness it and more,
The pomp of summer Days.

1659

Fame is a fickle food
Upon a shifting plate
Whose table once a
Guest but not
The second time is set.

Whose crumbs the crows inspect
And with ironic caw
Flap past it to the
Farmer's Corn —
Men eat of it and die.

1672

Lightly stepped a yellow star
To its lofty place —
Loosed the Moon her silver hat
From her lustral Face —
All of Evening softly lit
As an Astral Hall —
Father, I observed to Heaven,
You are punctual.

1715

Consulting summer's clock,
But half the hours remain.
I ascertain it with a shock —
I shall not look again.
The second half of joy
Is shorter than the first.
The truth I do not dare to know
I muffle with a jest.

1732

My life closed twice before its close —
It yet remains to see
If Immortality unveil
A third event to me

So huge, so hopeless to conceive
As these that twice befell.
Parting is all we know of heaven,
And all we need of hell.

WALLACE STEVENS

If Robert Frost is the modern poet most admired by the general public and William Carlos Williams the favorite of younger poets, Wallace Stevens is the undisputed champion of the academic establishment, the critic's poet. Preoccupied with "ideas of order" and convinced that the imagination can discover "the opposite of chaos in chaos," he is an ideal seminar artist, a philosophical writer whose richly textured lyrics, consistently revealing new meanings and tonalities, lend themselves to exhaustive classroom analysis. His poems, like Faulkner's novels, are fascinating puzzles that reward repeated visits, though they will frustrate anyone insisting on literal meanings. The late critic Anatole Broyard said that he survived his army years by keeping a copy of the poet with him at all times, and one is reminded of Emily Dickinson's question about Shakespeare: "Why is any other book needed?" Unlike Frost, Stevens is not for everyone, but those who do respond to his music tend to find him without peer among American singers.

While the poet's inner life was quite obviously rich, the biographical facts of his career could hardly be more ordinary. Wallace Stevens was not the sort of flamboyant artist who fires the imagination of playwrights or novelists looking for a likely subject; he was, rather, a singularly private man with few captivating personal quirks and no talent for self-promotion. His friend William Carlos Williams referred to "Dear fat Stevens" as "a veritable monk . . . drawing back from the world." Urbane, forbidding, almost Olympian (albeit with a caustic playfulness), he seemed more the meticulously tailored lawyer than a typically free-spirited artist.

A highly disciplined businessman, he felt that poets who held university positions and read to women's groups were "kept men." "I detest 'company,'" he said, "and do not fear any protest of selfishness in saying so." Some of his business associates, it is told, did not even know that he was a major literary figure, though such a story may be an exaggeration. ("We just accepted Wallace Stevens," a colleague said, "as another man in the office—smart as hell—who liked to write poetry.") The most remarkable thing about him, it seems, apart from his immense size (well over six feet tall and weighing nearly 250 pounds), is that there was nothing remarkable about him. "Have you anything to declare?" a customs official once asked Oscar Wilde. "No, I have nothing to declare," he responded, "except my genius."

There were no customs officials in Stevens's own life, since he was the rare American artist who never traveled abroad but instead experienced "the heaven of Europe" secondhand, through letters, postcards, art catalogues, wines, and other "authentic food for a starved imagination," to borrow Helen Vendler's apt words. Born of German-Dutch ancestry in Reading, Pennsylvania, in 1879, he spent three years at Harvard, studying French and German and serving as president of the *Harvard Advocate*, where his earliest poems appeared. After college he worked for *The New York Herald Tribune* and then, at the urging of his father, an attorney who wrote poetry, he attended the New York Law School. At twenty-five he was admitted to the bar and for the next twelve years practiced law, with little success, in New York. At thirty, after a long courtship, he married Elsie Kachel, a moody, socially awkward woman with a grammar school education who gained some fame in her own right as the model for the head on the Liberty Head dime. In proposing to her, Stevens asked, "Are you really fond of books—paper valleys and far countries, paper gardens, paper men and women? I live with them constantly." Though the couple remained together and raised a daughter, who would later help edit her father's work, the marriage, documented in several poems, was not made in heaven. In 1916 Stevens accepted a position with the Hartford Accident and Indemnity Company, where he remained for the rest of his life, having been named vice-president in 1934. Twenty-one years later, aged seventy-six, he died of cancer.

Stevens's first book, *Harmonium,* was not published until his forty-fourth year, though his work had been attracting admiration for nearly a decade in *Poetry* and other little magazines. It is just as well that he had another occupation—the book, which sold fewer than one hundred copies, earned him $6.70. A second volume, *Ideas of Order,* did not appear for another twelve years ("A book of poems," he said, "is a damned serious affair"), but through his appearances in literary magazines he continued to acquire an audience responsive to his meditative lyrics. Given to jotting notes for poems while he walked to work, he would dictate to his secretary and then revise at home in the evenings and on weekends, sometimes so absorbed that he missed meals.

In his late fifties he published two volumes—*Ideas of Order* (1935) and *The Man with the Blue Guitar* (1937)—that left no question about his importance. Continuing to produce steadily (nearly half of his work was written in his final decade), he devoted his leisure time to the other things he loved: trips to Key West (where he reputedly broke his hand in a fistfight with Ernest Hemingway), long walks, and his collections of paintings and classical records. He also enjoyed rare beef, strong martinis, risqué jokes, and Greta Garbo films. The recipient of various awards and honorary degrees, he never took such accolades very seriously. Returning from a Columbia University commencement in 1952, he hung up his bright new academic hood and said to his wife, "Look, darling, I have another scalp."

Stevens's *Collected Poems* was published to critical acclaim the year before his death, and an *Opus Posthumous* appeared three years later. "It is not what I have written," he said in accepting the National Book Award for *The Collected Poems*, "but what I would like to have written that constitutes my true poems." Those who are devoted to his work, especially to the pleasure of reading it aloud and basking in the harmonious music, even when it is not completely comprehensible, obviously feel otherwise.

BANTAMS IN PINE-WOODS

Chieftain Iffucan of Azcan in caftan
Of tan with henna hackles, halt!

Damned universal cock, as if the sun
Was blackamoor to bear your blazing tail.

Fat! Fat! Fat! Fat! I am the personal.
Your world is you. I am my world.

You ten-foot poet among inchlings. Fat!
Begone! An inchling bristles in these pines,

Bristles, and points their Appalachian tangs,
And fears not portly Azcan nor his hoos.

Poetry, in Stevens's mind, is "the supreme fiction," the single essence that can replace a lost belief in God as a source of life's redemption. "The greatest poverty," he wrote, "is not to live in a physical world." Obsessed with questions about the relations between reality and the imagination, he insisted that it is to the necessary fictions—that is, works of art, shaped by the imagination—that we must turn for "a freshening of life." Reality, he believed, is a cliché from which we escape by metaphor into a realm of wonder and delight.

The fantastic quality of his own metaphors, coupled with his voluptuary hedonism, has led some readers to charge Stevens with foppish affectation ("a stuffed goldfinch," one critic called him) and aesthetic dandyism. (Frost referred to him as "the bric-a-brac poet.") In a typical poem, ocean waves are likened to certain kinds of chocolate, to umbrellas, and to French phrases. Little wonder that Marianne Moore called him

"America's chief conjurer." But if the poems are characterized by exotic turns, dazzling in their virtuoso extravagance and unexpected comic vigor, they are also vehicles for rational meditation on significant questions. He was, in Delmore Schwartz's words, "an aesthete in the best sense of the word." "Yet in excess continual," Stevens wrote, "there is cure of sorrow." It is his rare combination of verbal acrobatics and serious intellectual probing that makes him at once the most puzzling, the most entertaining, and the most seductive of artists.

The Collected Poems of Wallace Stevens (Vintage Books, 1982). Peter Brazeau, *Parts of the World, Wallace Stevens Remembered* (North Point Press, 1985), an oral biography. For criticism, see Harold Bloom, *Wallace Stevens, The Poems of Our Climate* (Cornell University Press, 1977); A. Walton Litz, *Introspective Voyager: The Poetic Development of Wallace Stevens* (Oxford University Press, 1969); and Helen Vendler, *On Extended Wings: Wallace Stevens' Longer Poems* (Harvard University Press, 1969).

EARTHY ANECDOTE

Every time the bucks went clattering
Over Oklahoma
A firecat bristled in the way.

Wherever they went,
They went clattering,
Until they swerved

In a swift, circular line
To the right,
Because of the firecat.

Or until they swerved
In a swift, circular line
To the left,
Because of the firecat.

The bucks clattered.
The firecat went leaping,
To the right, to the left,
And
Bristled in the way.

Later, the firecat closed his bright eyes
And slept.

IN THE CAROLINAS

The lilacs wither in the Carolinas.
Already the butterflies flutter above the cabins.
Already the new-born children interpret love
In the voices of mothers.

Timeless mother,
How is it that your aspic nipples
For once vent honey?

The pine-tree sweetens my body
The white iris beautifies me.

The Plot Against the Giant

First Girl

When this yokel comes maundering,
Whetting his hacker,
I shall run before him,
Diffusing the civilest odors
Out of geraniums and unsmelled flowers.
It will check him.

Second Girl

I shall run before him,
Arching cloths besprinkled with colors
As small as fish-eggs.
The threads
Will abash him.

Third Girl

Oh, la . . . le pauvre!
I shall run before him,
With a curious puffing.
He will bend his ear then.
I shall whisper
Heavenly labials in a world of gutturals.
It will undo him.

Valley Candle

My candle burned alone in an immense valley.
Beams of the huge night converged upon it,
Until the wind blew.

Then beams of the huge night
Converged upon its image,
Until the wind blew.

DISILLUSIONMENT OF TEN O'CLOCK

The houses are haunted
By white night-gowns.
None are green,
Or purple with green rings,
Or green with yellow rings,
Or yellow with blue rings.
None of them are strange,
With socks of lace
And beaded ceintures.
People are not going
To dream of baboons and periwinkles.
Only, here and there, an old sailor,
Drunk and asleep in his boots,
Catches tigers
In red weather.

SUNDAY MORNING

I

Complacencies of the peignoir, and late
Coffee and oranges in a sunny chair,
And the green freedom of a cockatoo
Upon a rug mingle to dissipate
The holy hush of ancient sacrifice.
She dreams a little, and she feels the dark
Encroachment of that old catastrophe,
As a calm darkens among water-lights.

The pungent oranges and bright, green wings
Seem things in some procession of the dead,
Winding across wide water, without sound.
The day is like wide water, without sound,
Stilled for the passing of her dreaming feet
Over the seas, to silent Palestine,
Dominion of the blood and sepulchre.

II

Why should she give her bounty to the dead?
What is divinity if it can come
Only in silent shadows and in dreams?
Shall she not find in comforts of the sun,
In pungent fruit and bright, green wings, or else
In any balm or beauty of the earth,
Things to be cherished like the thought of heaven?
Divinity must live within herself:
Passions of rain, or moods in falling snow;
Grievings in loneliness, or unsubdued
Elations when the forest blooms; gusty
Emotions on wet roads on autumn nights;
All pleasures and all pains, remembering
The bough of summer and the winter branch.
These are the measures destined for her soul.

III

Jove in the clouds had his inhuman birth.
No mother suckled him, no sweet land gave
Large-mannered motions to his mythy mind
He moved among us, as a muttering king,
Magnificent, would move among his hinds,
Until our blood, commingling, virginal,

With heaven, brought such requital to desire
The very hinds discerned it, in a star.
Shall our blood fail? Or shall it come to be
The blood of paradise? And shall the earth
Seem all of paradise that we shall know?
The sky will be much friendlier then than now,
A part of labor and a part of pain,
And next in glory to enduring love,
Not this dividing and indifferent blue.

IV

She says, "I am content when wakened birds,
Before they fly, test the reality
Of misty fields, by their sweet questionings;
But when the birds are gone, and their warm fields
Return no more, where, then, is paradise?"
There is not any haunt of prophecy,
Nor any old chimera of the grave,
Neither the golden underground, nor isle
Melodious, where spirits gat them home,
Nor visionary south, nor cloudy palm
Remote on heaven's hill, that has endured
As April's green endures; or will endure
Like her remembrance of awakened birds,
Or her desire for June and evening, tipped
By the consummation of the swallow's wings.

V

She says, "But in contentment I still feel
The need of some imperishable bliss."
Death is the mother of beauty; hence from her,
Alone, shall come fulfilment to our dreams

And our desires. Although she strews the leaves
Of sure obliteration on our paths,
The path sick sorrow took, the many paths
Where triumph rang its brassy phrase, or love
Whispered a little out of tenderness,
She makes the willow shiver in the sun
For maidens who were wont to sit and gaze
Upon the grass, relinquished to their feet.
She causes boys to pile new plums and pears
On disregarded plate. The maidens taste
And stray impassioned in the littering leaves.

VI

Is there no change of death in paradise?
Does ripe fruit never fall? Or do the boughs
Hang always heavy in that perfect sky,
Unchanging, yet so like our perishing earth,
With rivers like our own that seek for seas
They never find, the same receding shores
That never touch with inarticulate pang?
Why set the pear upon those river-banks
Or spice the shores with odors of the plum?
Alas, that they should wear our colors there,
The silken weavings of our afternoons,
And pick the strings of our insipid lutes!
Death is the mother of beauty, mystical,
Within whose burning bosom we devise
Our earthly mothers waiting, sleeplessly.

VII

Supple and turbulent, a ring of men
Shall chant in orgy on a summer morn

Their boisterous devotion to the sun,
Not as a god, but as a god might be,
Naked among them, like a savage source.
Their chant shall be a chant of paradise,
Out of their blood, returning to the sky;
And in their chant shall enter, voice by voice,
The windy lake wherein their lord delights,
The trees, like serafin, and echoing hills,
That choir among themselves long afterward.
They shall know well the heavenly fellowship
Of men that perish and of summer morn.
And whence they came and whither they shall go
The dew upon their feet shall manifest.

VIII

She hears, upon that water without sound,
A voice that cries, "The tomb in Palestine
Is not the porch of spirits lingering.
It is the grave of Jesus, where he lay."
We live in an old chaos of the sun,
Or old dependency of day and night,
Or island solitude, unsponsored, free,
Of that wide water, inescapable.
Deer walk upon our mountains, and the quail
Whistle about us their spontaneous cries;
Sweet berries ripen in the wilderness;
And, in the isolation of the sky,
At evening, casual flocks of pigeons make
Ambiguous undulations as they sink,
Downward to darkness, on extended wings.

ANECDOTE OF THE JAR

I placed a jar in Tennessee,
And round it was, upon a hill.
It made the slovenly wilderness
Surround that hill.

The wilderness rose up to it,
And sprawled around, no longer wild.
The jar was round upon the ground
And tall and of a port in air.

It took dominion everywhere.
The jar was gray and bare.
It did not give of bird or bush,
Like nothing else in Tennessee.

LIFE IS MOTION

In Oklahoma,
Bonnie and Josie,
Dressed in calico,
Danced around a stump.
They cried,
"Ohoyaho,
Ohoo" . . .
Celebrating the marriage
Of flesh and air.

PETER QUINCE AT THE CLAVIER

I

Just as my fingers on these keys
Make music, so the selfsame sounds
On my spirit make a music, too.

Music is feeling, then, not sound;
And thus it is that what I feel,
Here in this room, desiring you,

Thinking of your blue-shadowed silk,
Is music. It is like the strain
Waked in the elders by Susanna.

Of a green evening, clear and warm,
She bathed in her still garden, while
The red-eyed elders watching, felt

The basses of their beings throb
In witching chords, and their thin blood
Pulse pizzicati of Hosanna.

II
In the green water, clear and warm,
Susanna lay.
She searched
The touch of springs,
And found
Concealed imaginings.
She sighed,
For so much melody.

Upon the bank, she stood
In the cool
Of spent emotions.
She felt, among the leaves,
The dew
Of old devotions.

She walked upon the grass,
Still quavering.

The winds were like her maids,
On timid feet,
Fetching her woven scarves,
Yet wavering.

A breath upon her hand
Muted the night.
She turned —
A cymbal crashed,
And roaring horns.

III

Soon, with a noise like tambourines,
Came her attendant Byzantines.

They wondered why Susanna cried
Against the elders by her side;

And as they whispered, the refrain
Was like a willow swept by rain.

Anon, their lamps' uplifted flame
Revealed Susanna and her shame.

And then, the simpering Byzantines
Fled, with a noise like tambourines.

IV

Beauty is momentary in the mind —
The fitful tracing of a portal;
But in the flesh it is immortal.
The body dies; the body's beauty lives.
So evenings die, in their green going,
A wave, interminably flowing.

So gardens die, their meek breath scenting
The cowl of winter, done repenting.
So maidens die, to the auroral
Celebration of a maiden's choral.
Susanna's music touched the bawdy strings
Of those white elders; but, escaping,
Left only Death's ironic scraping.
Now, in its immortality, it plays
On the clear viol of her memory,
And makes a constant sacrament of praise.

THIRTEEN WAYS OF LOOKING AT A BLACKBIRD

I

Among twenty snowy mountains,
The only moving thing
Was the eye of the blackbird.

II

I was of three minds,
Like a tree
In which there are three blackbirds.

III

The blackbird whirled in the autumn winds.
It was a small part of the pantomime.

IV

A man and a woman
Are one.
A man and a woman and a blackbird
Are one.

V

I do not know which to prefer,
The beauty of inflections
Or the beauty of innuendoes,
The blackbird whistling
Or just after.

VI

Icicles filled the long window
With barbaric glass.
The shadow of the blackbird
Crossed it, to and fro.
The mood
Traced in the shadow
An indecipherable cause.

VII

O thin men of Haddam,
Why do you imagine golden birds?
Do you not see how the blackbird
Walks around the feet
Of the women about you?

VIII

I know noble accents
And lucid, inescapable rhythms;
But I know, too,
That the blackbird is involved
In what I know.

IX

When the blackbird flew out of sight,
It marked the edge
Of one of many circles.

X

At the sight of blackbirds
Flying in a green light,
Even the bawds of euphony
Would cry out sharply.

XI

He rode over Connecticut
In a glass coach.
Once, a fear pierced him,
In that he mistook
The shadow of his equipage
For blackbirds.

XII

The river is moving.
The blackbird must be flying.

XIII

It was evening all afternoon.
It was snowing
And it was going to snow.
The blackbird sat
In the cedar-limbs.

WALLACE STEVENS   127

THE DEATH OF A SOLDIER

Life contracts and death is expected,
As in a season of autumn.
The soldier falls.

He does not become a three-days personage,
Imposing his separation,
Calling for pomp.

Death is absolute and without memorial,
As in a season of autumn,
When the wind stops,

When the wind stops and, over the heavens,
The clouds go, nevertheless,
In their direction.

LUNAR PARAPHRASE

The moon is the mother of pathos and pity.

When, at the wearier end of November,
Her old light moves along the branches,
Feebly, slowly, depending upon them;
When the body of Jesus hangs in a pallor,
Humanly near, and the figure of Mary,
Touched on by hoar-frost, shrinks in a shelter
Made by the leaves, that have rotted and fallen;
When over the houses, a golden illusion
Brings back an earlier season of quiet
And quieting dreams in the sleepers in darkness —

The moon is the mother of pathos and pity.

THE IDEA OF ORDER AT KEY WEST

She sang beyond the genius of the sea.
The water never formed to mind or voice,
Like a body wholly body, fluttering
Its empty sleeves; and yet its mimic motion
Made constant cry, caused constantly a cry,
That was not ours although we understood,
Inhuman, of the veritable ocean.

The sea was not a mask. No more was she.
The song and water were not medleyed sound
Even if what she sang was what she heard,
Since what she sang was uttered word by word.
It may be that in all her phrases stirred
The grinding water and the gasping wind;
But it was she and not the sea we heard.

For she was the maker of the song she sang.
The ever-hooded, tragic-gestured sea
Was merely a place by which she walked to sing.
Whose spirit is this? we said, because we knew
It was the spirit that we sought and knew
That we should ask this often as she sang.

If it was only the dark voice of the sea
That rose, or even colored by many waves;
If it was only the outer voice of sky
And cloud, of the sunken coral water-walled,
However clear, it would have been deep air,
The heaving speech of air, a summer sound

Repeated in a summer without end
And sound alone. But it was more than that,
More even than her voice, and ours, among
The meaningless plungings of water and the wind,
Theatrical distances, bronze shadows heaped
On high horizons, mountainous atmospheres
Of sky and sea.

                    It was her voice that made
The sky acutest at its vanishing.
She measured to the hour its solitude.
She was the single artificer of the world
In which she sang. And when she sang, the sea,
Whatever self it had, became the self
That was her song, for she was the maker. Then we,
As we beheld her striding there alone,
Knew that there never was a world for her
Except the one she sang and, singing, made.

Ramon Fernandez, tell me, if you know,
Why, when the singing ended and we turned
Toward the town, tell why the glassy lights,
The lights in the fishing boats at anchor there,
As the night descended, tilting in the air,
Mastered the night and portioned out the sea,
Fixing emblazoned zones and fiery poles,
Arranging, deepening, enchanting night.

Oh! Blessed rage for order, pale Ramon,
The maker's rage to order words of the sea,
Words of the fragrant portals, dimly-starred,
And of ourselves and of our origins,
In ghostlier demarcations, keener sounds.

THE BRAVE MAN

The sun, that brave man,
Comes through boughs that lie in wait,
That brave man.

Green and gloomy eyes
In dark forms of the grass
Run away.

The good stars,
Pale helms and spiky spurs,
Run away.

Fears of my bed,
Fears of life and fears of death,
Run away.

That brave man comes up
From below and walks without meditation,
That brave man.

GRAY STONES AND GRAY PIGEONS

The archbishop is away. The church is gray.
He has left his robes folded in camphor
And, dressed in black, he walks
Among fireflies.

The bony buttresses, the bony spires
Arranged under the stony clouds
Stand in a fixed light.
The bishop rests.

He is away. The church is gray.
This is his holiday.
The sexton moves with a sexton's stare
In the air.

A dithery gold falls everywhere.
It wets the pigeons,
It goes and the birds go,
Turn dry,

Birds that never fly
Except when the bishop passes by,
Globed in today and tomorrow,
Dressed in his colored robes.

THE READER

All night I sat reading a book,
Sat reading as if in a book
Of sombre pages.

It was autumn and falling stars
Covered the shrivelled forms
Crouched in the moonlight.

No lamp was burning as I read,
A voice was mumbling, "Everything
Falls back to coldness,

Even the musky muscadines,
The melons, the vermilion pears
Of the leafless garden."

The sombre pages bore no print
Except the trace of burning stars
In the frosty heaven.

ANGLAIS MORT À FLORENCE

A little less returned for him each spring.
Music began to fail him. Brahms, although
His dark familiar, often walked apart.

His spirit grew uncertain of delight,
Certain of its uncertainty, in which
That dark companion left him unconsoled

For a self returning mostly memory.
Only last year he said that the naked moon
Was not the moon he used to see, to feel

(In the pale coherences of moon and mood
When he was young), naked and alien,
More leanly shining from a lankier sky.

Its ruddy pallor had grown cadaverous.
He used his reason, exercised his will,
Turning in time to Brahms as alternate

In speech. He was that music and himself.
They were particles of order, a single majesty:
But he remembered the time when he stood alone.

He stood at last by God's help and the police;
But he remembered the time when he stood alone.
He yielded himself to that single majesty;

But he remembered the time when he stood alone,
When to be and delight to be seemed to be one,
Before the colors deepened and grew small.

A Postcard from the Volcano

Children picking up our bones
Will never know that these were once
As quick as foxes on the hill;

And that in autumn, when the grapes
Made sharp air sharper by their smell
These had a being, breathing frost;

And least will guess that with our bones
We left much more, left what still is
The look of things, left what we felt

At what we saw. The spring clouds blow
Above the shuttered mansion-house,
Beyond our gate and the windy sky.

Cries out a literate despair.
We knew for long the mansion's look
And what we said of it became

A part of what it is . . . Children,
Still weaving budded aureoles,
Will speak our speech and never know,

Will say of the mansion that it seems
As if he that lived there left behind
A spirit storming in blank walls,

A dirty house in a gutted world,
A tatter of shadows peaked to white,
Smeared with the gold of the opulent sun.

ON THE ADEQUACY OF LANDSCAPE

The little owl flew through the night,
As if the people in the air
Were frightened and he frightened them,
By being there,

The people that turned off and came
To avoid the bright, discursive wings,
To avoid the hap-hallow hallow-ho
Of central things,

Nor in their empty hearts to feel
The blood-red redness of the sun,
To shrink to an insensible,
Small oblivion,

Beyond the keenest diamond day
Of people sensible to pain,
When cocks wake, clawing at their beds
To be again,

And who, for that, turn toward the cocks
And toward the start of day and trees
And light behind the body of night
And sun, as if these

Were what they are, the sharpest sun:
The sharpest self, the sensible range,
The extent of what they are, the strength
That they exchange,

So that he that suffers most desires
The red bird most and the strongest sky —
Not the people in the air that hear
The little owl fly.

Contrary Theses (I)

Now grapes are plush upon the vines.
A soldier walks before my door.

The hives are heavy with the combs.
Before, before, before my door.

And seraphs cluster on the domes,
And saints are brilliant in fresh cloaks.

Before, before, before my door.
The shadows lessen on the walls.

The bareness of the house returns.
An acid sunlight fills the halls.

Before, before. Blood smears the oaks.
A soldier stalks before my door.

God Is Good. It Is a Beautiful Night

Look round, brown moon, brown bird, as you rise to fly,
Look round at the head and zither
On the ground.

Look round you as you start to rise, brown moon,
At the book and shoe, the rotted rose
At the door.

This was the place to which you came last night,
Flew close to, flew to without rising away.
Now, again,

In your light, the head is speaking. It reads the book.
It becomes the scholar again, seeking celestial
Rendezvous,

Picking thin music on the rustiest string,
Squeezing the reddest fragrance from the stump
Of summer.

The venerable song falls from your fiery wings.
The song of the great space of your age pierces
The fresh night.

FLYER'S FALL

This man escaped the dirty fates,
Knowing that he died nobly, as he died.

Darkness, nothingness of human after-death,
Receive and keep him in the deepnesses of space —

Profundum, physical thunder, dimension in which
We believe without belief, beyond belief.

DEBRIS OF LIFE AND MIND

There is so little that is close and warm.
It is as if we were never children.

Sit in the room. It is true in the moonlight
That it is as if we had never been young.

We ought not to be awake. It is from this
That a bright red woman will be rising

And, standing in violent golds, will brush her hair.
She will speak thoughtfully the words of a line.

She will think about them not quite able to sing.
Besides, when the sky is so blue, things sing themselves,

Even for her, already for her. She will listen
And feel that her color is a meditation,

The most gay and yet not so gay as it was.
Stay here. Speak of familiar things a while.

THINKING OF A RELATION BETWEEN
THE IMAGES OF METAPHORS

The wood-doves are singing along the Perkiomen.
The bass lie deep, still afraid of the Indians.

In the one ear of the fisherman, who is all
One ear, the wood-doves are singing a single song.

The bass keep looking ahead, upstream, in one
Direction, shrinking from the spit and splash

Of waterish spears. The fisherman is all
One eye, in which the dove resembles the dove.

There is one dove, one bass, one fisherman.
Yet coo becomes rou-coo, rou-coo. How close

To the unstated theme each variation comes . . .
In that one ear it might strike perfectly:

State the disclosure. In that one eye the dove
Might spring to sight and yet remain a dove.

The fisherman might be the single man
In whose breast, the dove, alighting, would grow
    still.

THE HOUSE WAS QUIET
AND THE WORLD WAS CALM

The house was quiet and the world was calm.
The reader became the book; and summer night

Was like the conscious being of the book.
The house was quiet and the world was calm.

The words were spoken as if there was no book,
Except that the reader leaned above the page,

Wanted to lean, wanted much most to be
The scholar to whom his book is true, to whom

The summer night is like a perfection of thought.
The house was quiet because it had to be.

The quiet was part of the meaning, part of the mind:
The access of perfection to the page.

And the world was calm. The truth in a calm world,
In which there is no other meaning, itself

Is calm, itself is summer and night, itself
Is the reader leaning late and reading there.

VACANCY IN THE PARK

March . . . Someone has walked across the snow,
Someone looking for he knows not what.

It is like a boat that has pulled away
From a shore at night and disappeared.

It is like a guitar left on a table
By a woman, who has forgotten it.

It is like the feeling of a man
Come back to see a certain house.

The four winds blow through the rustic arbor,
Under its mattresses of vines.

SONG OF FIXED ACCORD

Rou-cou spoke the dove,
Like the sooth lord of sorrow,
Of sooth love and sorrow,
And a hail-bow, hail-bow,
To this morrow.

She lay upon the roof,
A little wet of wing and woe,
And she rou-ed there,
Softly she piped among the suns
And their ordinary glare,

The sun of five, the sun of six,
Their ordinariness,
And the ordinariness of seven,
Which she accepted,
Like a fixed heaven,

Not subject to change . . .
Day's invisible beginner,
The lord of love and of sooth sorrow,
Lay on the roof
And made much within her.

The Planet on the Table

Ariel was glad he had written his poems.
They were of a remembered time
Or of something seen that he liked.

Other makings of the sun
Were waste and welter
And the ripe shrub writhed.

His self and the sun were one
And his poems, although makings of his self,
Were no less makings of the sun.

It was not important that they survive.
What mattered was that they should bear
Some lineament or character,

Some affluence, if only half-perceived,
In the poverty of their words,
Of the planet of which they were part.

Not Ideas About the Thing but the Thing Itself

At the earliest ending of winter,
In March, a scrawny cry from outside
Seemed like a sound in his mind.

He knew that he heard it,
A bird's cry, at daylight or before,
In the early March wind.

The sun was rising at six,
No longer a battered panache above snow . . .
It would have been outside.

It was not from the vast ventriloquism
Of sleep's faded papier-mâché . . .
The sun was coming from outside.

That scrawny cry — it was
A chorister whose c preceded the choir.
It was part of the colossal sun,

Surrounded by its choral rings,
Still far away. It was like
A new knowledge of reality.

WILLIAM CARLOS WILLIAMS

The critic Randall Jarrell had compelling reasons for calling William Carlos Williams "the America of poets." Resisting the temptation to join such compatriots as T. S. Eliot and Ezra Pound in European exile, Williams spent virtually his entire seventy-nine years in the provincial New Jersey town where he was born. His work, whether poetry, fiction, nonfiction, or drama, deals with American subjects and settings and does so in the vernacular language that he favored over a more formal rhetoric drawn from European models—"noble has been / changed to no bull." In *Paterson,* his ambitious poetic sequence, he attempted to provide a microcosm of his country's history, and it is not farfetched to say that with an international mix of blood in his veins this child of immigrant parents was himself an American microcosm—his father was born in England and his mother (Raquel Helene Rose Hobeb Williams), of Dutch, Spanish, and Jewish descent, in Puerto Rico.

"Of mixed ancestry," he wrote, "I felt from earliest childhood that America was the only home I could ever call my own. I felt that it was expressly founded for me, personally, and that it must be my first business in life to possess it; that only by making it my own from the beginning to my own day, in detail, should I ever have a basis for knowing where I stood." At the center of all Williams's work is a robust delight in this possibility of possessing his country, past and present, as a means of perpetually renewing himself and of discovering his own potential humanity.

Only by living in a place, he believed, could one imaginatively possess it ("the local is the universal"), and so at a time when other writers were turning their backs on the New World in favor of older cultures, he chose to dig in what Ezra Pound called "the bloody loam," chose to use the imagination and the spoken language to lift his own environment to the sphere of the intelligence. He was determined to discover a culture as "locally related" as a tree in the earth. Pound astutely referred to this Daniel Boone of letters as "the observant foreigner, perceiving American vegetation and landscape quite directly, as something put there for him to look at." Williams was a keen-eyed observer who described what he saw in words that, as Marianne Moore nicely put it, dogs and cats can understand. The commonplace, the tawdry, even the sordid, he said, all have their poetic uses if the imagination can lighten them.

Meanwhile,
the old man who goes about
gathering dog-lime
walks in the gutter
without looking up
and his tread
is more majestic than
that of the Episcopal minister
approaching the pulpit
of a Sunday.
These things
astonish me beyond words.

The poet was born September 17, 1883, in Rutherford,
New Jersey. After Horace Mann School in New York he
attended the University of Pennsylvania, studying first dentis-
try and then medicine. While there he formed a close relation-
ship with classmate Ezra Pound, who was to be a friendly
antagonist for the next fifty years—Williams respected his
friend's art but despised his politics, especially his anti-
Semitism. Following his internship in New York and a period
of European study and travel he settled down for good in
Rutherford. In 1912 he married Florence Herman, the "Flos-
sie" of his poems, a tough-minded woman who remained a
support throughout his life and a devoted mother to their two
sons despite the poet's infidelities. "Do you want to make love
to every single woman you meet?" an interviewer once asked
him. "Yes," came the grave reply, "I do."

For the next fifty years Williams lived the equivalent of
several lives. As a pediatrician and obstetrician he carried on

a full-time practice, which included delivering over two thousand babies; at the same time, writing poems on prescription blanks during free moments, he somehow managed to become the most influential and original poet of the century. He also found the energy to write novels, books of stories, plays, essays, and a remarkable meditation on history, *In the American Grain*. His scientific insistence on accuracy proved troublesome at one point when he was sued for using actual names in a story published in *New Masses*. He eventually settled out of court for five thousand dollars, a considerable sum in 1926.

In his late sixties the poet suffered a series of strokes that forced him to give up his medical practice (one of his sons took it over) and made writing difficult. Having lost the use of his right arm, he stubbornly learned to type with his left hand. At one point, when he was seventy, he was hospitalized for a severe depression, brought about in part by the nightmare experience of having a promised appointment as Consultant in Poetry at the Library of Congress sabotaged by an obscure McCarthyite who, referring to the poet as "the very voice of Communism," leveled a number of preposterous charges against him. The tenacious old man persevered, however, and in his final years wrote the beautiful fifth book of *Paterson*, as well as *Pictures from Brueghel and Other Poems*, which won a Pulitzer Prize.

That this prize was awarded posthumously is telling: Williams's reputation never really caught up with him during his lifetime, despite the breadth and excellence of his work. At the time of his death in 1963 his public was small and university critics had only just begun to turn him into a kind of academic growth industry. He had no illusions about fame, as indicated by some words he wrote, at seventy-two, about a postcard sent by a friend: "It shows four old musicians walking poorly clad in the snow. . . . They are all scrunched together their instruments in their hands trudging along. I mean to keep the card there a long time as a reminder of our probable fate as artists. I know just what is going on in the minds of these white haired musicians."

In recent years the reputation of this white-haired musician, this "man on the margin," as one critic called him, has risen steadily. At one time a British reviewer could dismiss him as "a writer of some local interest, perhaps." Now Williams has come to be universally regarded as one of the most significant American poets since Whitman. In addition to the innate importance of his own work, he has influenced countless younger artists, including Denise Levertov, Robert Creeley, Kenneth Rexroth, Robert Lowell, and, especially, Allen Ginsberg. Rutherford was for years a place of pilgrimage for young writers, and the poet's personal generosity, coupled with his revolutionary approach to poetic language, made him the father figure to an entire generation of nonacademic American poets. Typically, he discouraged his poetic heirs from referring to him as "father" or "maestro."

The Collected Poems of William Carlos Williams, edited by A. Walton Litz and Christopher MacGowan. Volume 1, *1909–1939* (New Directions, 1986); Volume 2, *1939–1962* (New Directions, 1988). For biographical information, see Paul Mariani, *William Carlos Williams: A New World Naked*

(W. W. Norton, paperback, 1990). For criticism, see James
Breslin, *William Carlos Williams, An American Artist* (Oxford
University Press, 1970); Randall Jarrell, ed., *The Selected Poems
of William Carlos Williams* (New Directions, 1963); and
Thomas R. Whitaker, *William Carlos Williams* (Twayne Pub-
lishers, 1968).

MEZZO FORTE

Take that, damn you; and that!
    And here's a rose
    To make it right again!
    God knows
    I'm sorry, Grace; but then,
It's not my fault if you will be a cat.

THE REVELATION

I awoke happy, the house
Was strange, voices
Were across a gap
Through which a girl
Came and paused,
Reaching out to me —

Then I remembered
What I had dreamed —
A girl
One whom I knew well
Leaned on the door of my car
And stroked my hand —

I shall pass her on the street
We shall say trivial things
To each other
But I shall never cease
To search her eyes
For that quiet look —

PASTORAL

When I was younger
it was plain to me
I must make something of myself.
Older now
I walk back streets
admiring the houses
of the very poor:
roof out of line with sides
the yards cluttered
with old chicken wire, ashes,
furniture gone wrong;
the fences and outhouses
built of barrel-staves
and parts of boxes, all,
if I am fortunate,
smeared a bluish green
that properly weathered
pleases me best
of all colors.
                    No one
will believe this
of vast import to the nation.

WILLIAM CARLOS WILLIAMS   151

APOLOGY

Why do I write today?

The beauty of
the terrible faces
of our nonentities
stirs me to it:

colored women
day workers —
old and experienced —
returning home at dusk
in cast off clothing
faces like
old Florentine oak.

Also

the set pieces
of your faces stir me —
leading citizens —
but not
in the same way.

PASTORAL

The little sparrows
hop ingenuously
about the pavement
quarreling
with sharp voices
over those things
that interest them.

But we who are wiser
shut ourselves in
on either hand
and no one knows
whether we think good
or evil.
          Meanwhile,
the old man who goes about
gathering dog-lime
walks in the gutter
without looking up
and his tread
is more majestic than
that of the Episcopal minister
approaching the pulpit
of a Sunday.
          These things
astonish me beyond words.

TRACT

I will teach you my townspeople
how to perform a funeral —
for you have it over a troop
of artists —
unless one should scour the world —
you have the ground sense necessary.

See! the hearse leads.
I begin with a design for a hearse.
For Christ's sake not black —
nor white either — and not polished!

Let it be weathered — like a farm wagon —
with gilt wheels (this could be
applied fresh at small expense)
or no wheels at all:
a rough dray to drag over the ground.

Knock the glass out!
My God — glass, my townspeople!
For what purpose? Is it for the dead
to look out or for us to see
how well he is housed or to see
the flowers or the lack of them —
or what?
To keep the rain and snow from him?
He will have a heavier rain soon:
pebbles and dirt and what not.
Let there be no glass —
and no upholstery, phew!
and no little brass rollers
and small easy wheels on the bottom —
my townspeople what are you thinking of?

A rough plain hearse then
with gilt wheels and no top at all.
On this the coffin lies
by its own weight.

                    No wreaths please —
especially no hot house flowers.
Some common memento is better,
something he prized and is known by:
his old clothes — a few books perhaps —

God knows what! You realize
how we are about these things
my townspeople —
something will be found — anything
even flowers if he had come to that.
So much for the hearse.

For heaven's sake though see to the driver!
Take off the silk hat! In fact
that's no place at all for him —
up there unceremoniously
dragging our friend out to his own dignity!
Bring him down — bring him down!
Low and inconspicuous! I'd not have him ride
on the wagon at all — damn him —
the undertaker's understrapper!
Let him hold the reins
and walk at the side
and inconspicuously too!

Then briefly as to yourselves:
Walk behind — as they do in France,
seventh class, or if you ride
Hell take curtains! Go with some show
of inconvenience; sit openly —
to the weather as to grief.
Or do you think you can shut grief in?
What — from us? We who have perhaps
nothing to lose? Share with us
share with us — it will be money
in your pockets.
                    Go now
I think you are ready.

El Hombre

It's a strange courage
you give me ancient star:

Shine alone in the sunrise
toward which you lend no part!

Mujer

Oh, black Persian cat!
Was not your life
already cursed with offspring?
We took you for rest to that old
Yankee farm, — so lonely
and with so many field mice
in the long grass —
and you return to us
in this condition — !

Oh, black Persian cat.

Love Song

Sweep the house clean,
hang fresh curtains
in the windows
put on a new dress
and come with me!
The elm is scattering
its little loaves
of sweet smells
from a white sky!

Who shall hear of us
in the time to come?
Let him say there was
a burst of fragrance
from black branches.

GOOD NIGHT

In brilliant gas light
I turn the kitchen spigot
and watch the water plash
into the clean white sink.
On the grooved drain-board
to one side is
a glass filled with parsley —
crisped green.

                Waiting
for the water to freshen —
I glance at the spotless floor — :
a pair of rubber sandals
lie side by side
under the wall-table
all is in order for the night.

Waiting, with a glass in my hand
  — three girls in crimson satin
pass close before me on
the murmurous background of
the crowded opera —

                    it is
memory playing the clown —
three vague, meaningless girls
full of smells and

the rustling sound of
cloth rubbing on cloth and
little slippers on carpet —
high-school French
spoken in a loud voice!

Parsley in a glass,
still and shining,
brings me back. I take my drink
and yawn deliciously.
I am ready for bed.

DANSE RUSSE

If I when my wife is sleeping
and the baby and Kathleen
are sleeping
and the sun is a flame-white disc
in silken mists
above shining trees, —
if I in my north room
dance naked, grotesquely
before my mirror
waving my shirt round my head
and singing softly to myself:
"I am lonely, lonely.
I was born to be lonely,
I am best so!"
If I admire my arms, my face,
my shoulders, flanks, buttocks
against the yellow drawn shades, —

Who shall say I am not
the happy genius of my household?

SMELL!

Oh strong-ridged and deeply hollowed
nose of mine! what will you not be smelling?
What tactless asses we are, you and I, boney nose,
always indiscriminate, always unashamed,
and now it is the souring flowers of the bedraggled
poplars: a festering pulp on the wet earth
beneath them. With what deep thirst
we quicken our desires
to that rank odor of a passing springtime!
Can you not be decent? Can you not reserve your ardors
for something less unlovely? What girl will care
for us, do you think, if we continue in these ways?
Must you taste everything? Must you know everything?
Must you have a part in everything?

THE YOUNG LAUNDRYMAN

Ladies, I crave your indulgence for
My friend Wu Kee; young, agile, clear-eyed
And clean-limbed, his muscles ripple
Under the thin blue shirt; and his naked feet, in
Their straw sandals, lift at the heels, shift and
Find new postures continually.

Your husband's shirts to wash, please, for Wu Kee.

TO MARK ANTHONY IN HEAVEN

This quiet morning light
reflected, how many times
from grass and trees and clouds
enters my north room

touching the walls with
grass and clouds and trees.
Anthony,
trees and grass and clouds.
Why did you follow
that beloved body
with your ships at Actium?
I hope it was because
you knew her inch by inch
from slanting feet upward
to the roots of her hair
and down again and that
you saw her
above the battle's fury —
clouds and trees and grass —

For then you are
listening in heaven.

THE LATE SINGER

Here it is spring again
and I still a young man!
I am late at my singing.
The sparrow with the black rain on his breast
has been at his cadenzas for two weeks past:
What is it that is dragging at my heart?
The grass by the back door
is stiff with sap.
The old maples are opening
their branches of brown and yellow moth-flowers.
A moon hangs in the blue
in the early afternoons over the marshes.
I am late at my singing.

COMPLAINT

They call me and I go.
It is a frozen road
past midnight, a dust
of snow caught
in the rigid wheeltracks.
The door opens.
I smile, enter and
shake off the cold.
Here is a great woman
on her side in the bed.
She is sick,
perhaps vomiting;
perhaps laboring
to give birth to
a tenth child. Joy! Joy!
Night is a room
darkened for lovers,
through the jealousies the sun
has sent one gold needle!
I pick the hair from her eyes
and watch her misery
with compassion.

COMPLETE DESTRUCTION

It was an icy day.
We buried the cat,
then took her box
and set match to it

in the back yard.
Those fleas that escaped
earth and fire
died by the cold.

WAITING

When I am alone I am happy.
The air is cool. The sky is
flecked and splashed and wound
with color. The crimson phalloi
of the sassafras leaves
hang crowded before me
in shoals on the heavy branches.
When I reach my doorstep
I am greeted by
the happy shrieks of my children
and my heart sinks.
I am crushed.

Are not my children as dear to me
as falling leaves or
must one become stupid
to grow older?
It seems much as if Sorrow
had tripped up my heels.
Let us see, let us see!
What did I plan to say to her
when it should happen to me
as it has happened now?

The Widow's Lament in Springtime

Sorrow is my own yard
where the new grass
flames as it has flamed
often before but not
with the cold fire
that closes round me this year.
Thirtyfive years
I lived with my husband.
The plumtree is white today
with masses of flowers.
Masses of flowers
load the cherry branches
and color some bushes
yellow and some red
but the grief in my heart
is stronger than they
for though they were my joy
formerly, today I notice them
and turn away forgetting.
Today my son told me
that in the meadows,
at the edge of the heavy woods
in the distance, he saw
trees of white flowers.
I feel that I would like
to go there
and fall into those flowers
and sink into the marsh near them.

THE GREAT FIGURE

Among the rain
and lights
I saw the figure 5
in gold
on a red
firetruck
moving
tense
unheeded
to gong clangs
siren howls
and wheels rumbling
through the dark city.

From SPRING AND ALL

This is the time of year
when boys fifteen and seventeen
wear two horned lilac blossoms
in their caps — or over one ear

What is it that does this?

It is a certain sort —
drivers for grocers or taxidrivers
white and colored —

fellows that let their hair grow long
in a curve over one eye —

Horned purple

Dirty satyrs, it is
vulgarity raised to the last power

They have stolen them
broken the bushes apart
with a curse for the owner —

Lilacs —

They stand in the doorways
on the business streets with a sneer
on their faces

adorned with blossoms

Out of their sweet heads
dark kisses — rough faces

From SPRING AND ALL

so much depends
upon

a red wheel
barrow

glazed with rain
water

beside the white
chickens

THE SEA-ELEPHANT

Trundled from
the strangeness of the sea —
a kind of
heaven —

Ladies and Gentlemen!
the greatest
sea-monster ever exhibited
alive

the gigantic
sea-elephant! O wallow
of flesh where
are

there fish enough for
that
appetite stupidity
cannot lessen?

Sick
of April's smallness
the little
leaves —

Flesh has lief of you
enormous sea —
Speak!
Blouaugh! (feed

me) my
flesh is riven —
fish after fish into his maw
unswallowing

to let them glide down
gulching back
half spittle half
brine

the
troubled eyes — torn
from the sea.
(In

a practical voice) They
ought
to put it back where
it came from.

Gape.
Strange head —
told by old sailors —
rising

bearded
to the surface — and
the only
sense out of them

is that woman's
Yes
it's wonderful but they
ought to

put it
back into the sea where
it came from.
Blouaugh!

Swing — ride
walk
on wires — toss balls
stoop and

contort yourselves —
But I
am love. I am
from the sea —

Blouaugh!
there is no crime save
the too-heavy
body

the sea
held playfully — comes
to the surface
the water

boiling
about the head the cows
scattering
fish dripping from

the bounty
of . . . . and spring
they say
Spring is icummen in —

Proletarian Portrait

A big young bareheaded woman
in an apron

Her hair slicked back standing
on the street

One stockinged foot toeing
the sidewalk

Her shoe in her hand. Looking
intently into it

She pulls out the paper insole
to find the nail

That has been hurting her

THE YACHTS

contend in a sea which the land partly encloses
shielding them from the too-heavy blows
of an ungoverned ocean which when it chooses

tortures the biggest hulls, the best man knows
to pit against its beatings, and sinks them pitilessly.
Mothlike in mists, scintillant in the minute

brilliance of cloudless days, with broad bellying sails
they glide to the wind tossing green water
from their sharp prows while over them the crew crawls

ant-like, solicitously grooming them, releasing,
making fast as they turn, lean far over and having
caught the wind again, side by side, head for the mark.

In a well guarded arena of open water surrounded by
lesser and greater craft which, sycophant, lumbering
and flittering follow them, they appear youthful, rare

as the light of a happy eye, live with the grace
of all that in the mind is feckless, free and
naturally to be desired. Now the sea which holds them

is moody, lapping their glossy sides, as if feeling
for some slightest flaw but fails completely.
Today no race. Then the wind comes again. The yachts

move, jockeying for a start, the signal is set and they
are off. Now the waves strike at them but they are too
well made, they slip through, though they take in canvas.

Arms with hands grasping seek to clutch at the prows.
Bodies thrown recklessly in the way are cut aside.
It is a sea of faces about them in agony, in despair

until the horror of the race dawns staggering the mind,
the whole sea become an entanglement of watery bodies
lost to the world bearing what they cannot hold. Broken,

beaten, desolate, reaching from the dead to be taken up
they cry out, failing, failing! their cries rising
in waves still as the skillful yachts pass over.

THE CATHOLIC BELLS

Tho' I'm no Catholic
I listen hard when the bells
in the yellow-brick tower
of their new church

ring down the leaves
ring in the frost upon them
and the death of the flowers
ring out the grackle

toward the south, the sky
darkened by them, ring in
the new baby of Mr. and Mrs.
Krantz which cannot

for the fat of its cheeks
open well its eyes, ring out

the parrot under its hood
jealous of the child

ring in Sunday morning
and old age which adds as it
takes away. Let them ring
only ring! over the oil

painting of a young priest
on the church wall advertising
last week's Novena to St.
Anthony, ring for the lame

young man in black with
gaunt cheeks and wearing a
Derby hat, who is hurrying
to 11 o'clock Mass (the

grapes still hanging to
the vines along the nearby
Concordia Halle like broken
teeth in the head of an

old man) Let them ring
for the eyes and ring for
the hands and ring for
the children of my friend

who no longer hears
them ring but with a smile
and in a low voice speaks
of the decisions of her

daughter and the proposals
and betrayals of her
husband's friends. O bells
ring for the ringing!

the beginning and the end
of the ringing! Ring ring
ring ring ring ring ring!
Catholic bells — !

BREAKFAST

Twenty sparrows
on

a scattered
turd:

Share and share
alike.

TO GREET A LETTER-CARRIER

Why'n't you bring me
a good letter? One with
lots of money in it.
I could make use of that.
Atta boy! Atta boy!

THE LAST WORDS OF
MY ENGLISH GRANDMOTHER

There were some dirty plates
and a glass of milk
beside her on a small table
near the rank, disheveled bed —

Wrinkled and nearly blind
she lay and snored

rousing with anger in her tones
to cry for food,

Gimme something to eat —
They're starving me —
I'm all right I won't go
to the hospital. No, no, no

Give me something to eat
Let me take you
to the hospital, I said
and after you are well

you can do as you please.
She smiled, Yes
you do what you please first
then I can do what I please —

Oh, oh, oh! she cried
as the ambulance men lifted
her to the stretcher —
Is this what you call

making me comfortable?
By now her mind was clear —
Oh you think you're smart
you young people,

she said, but I'll tell you
you don't know anything.
Then we started.
On the way

we passed a long row
of elms. She looked at them
awhile out of
the ambulance window and said,

What are all those
fuzzy-looking things out there?
Trees? Well, I'm tired
of them and rolled her head away.

THE DANCE

In Brueghel's great picture, The Kermess,
the dancers go round, they go round and
around, the squeal and the blare and the
tweedle of bagpipes, a bugle and fiddles
tipping their bellies (round as the thick-
sided glasses whose wash they impound)
their hips and their bellies off balance
to turn them. Kicking and rolling about
the Fair Grounds, swinging their butts, those
shanks must be sound to bear up under such
rollicking measures, prance as they dance
in Brueghel's great picture, The Kermess.

PRELUDE TO WINTER

The moth under the eaves
with wings like
the bark of a tree, lies
symmetrically still —

And love is a curious
soft-winged thing
unmoving under the eaves
when the leaves fall.

SILENCE

Under a low sky —
this quiet morning
of red and
yellow leaves —

a bird disturbs
no more than one twig
of the green leaved
peach tree

THE ACT

There were the roses, in the rain.
Don't cut them, I pleaded.
         They won't last, she said.
But they're so beautiful
      where they are.
Agh, we were all beautiful once, she
      said,
and cut them and gave them to me
      in my hand.

TO CLOSE

Will you please rush down and see
ma baby. You know, the one I talked
to you about last night

What was that?

WILLIAM CARLOS WILLIAMS   175

Is this the baby specialist?

Yes, but perhaps you mean my son,
can't you wait until   .   ?

I, I, I don't think it's brEAthin'

From THE DESCENT

The descent beckons
                as the ascent beckoned.
                        Memory is a kind
of accomplishment,
                a sort of renewal
                        even
an initiation, since the spaces it opens are new places
                inhabited by hordes
                        heretofore unrealized,
of new kinds —
                since their movements
                        are toward new objectives
(even though formerly they were abandoned).

No defeat is made up entirely of defeat — since
the world it opens is always a place
                formerly
                        unsuspected. A
world lost,
                a world unsuspected,
                        beckons to new places
and no whiteness (lost) is so white as the memory
of whiteness   .

With evening, love wakens
            though its shadows
                        which are alive by reason
of the sun shining —
            grow sleepy now and drop away
                        from desire   .

Love without shadows stirs now
            beginning to awaken
                        as night
advances.

The descent
            made up of despairs
                        and without accomplishment
realizes a new awakening:
                        which is a reversal
of despair.
            For what we cannot accomplish, what
is denied to love,
            what we have lost in the anticipation —
                        a descent follows,
endless and indestructible   .

To a Dog Injured in the Street

It is myself,
            not the poor beast lying there
                        yelping with pain
that brings me to myself with a start —
            as at the explosion
                        of a bomb, a bomb that has laid

all the world waste.
              I can do nothing
                         but sing about it
and so I am assuaged
              from my pain.

A drowsy numbness drowns my sense
              as if of hemlock
                         I had drunk. I think
of the poetry
              of René Char
                         and all he must have seen
and suffered
              that has brought him
                         to speak only of
sedgy rivers,
              of daffodils and tulips
                         whose roots they water,
even to the free-flowing river
              that laves the rootlets
                         of those sweet-scented flowers
that people the
              milky
                         way   .

I remember Norma
              our English setter of my childhood
                         her silky ears
and expressive eyes.
              She had a litter
                         of pups one night
in our pantry and I kicked
              one of them
                         thinking, in my alarm,

that they
            were biting her breasts
                        to destroy her.

I remember also
            a dead rabbit
                        lying harmlessly
on the outspread palm
            of a hunter's hand.
                        As I stood by
watching
            he took a hunting knife
                        and with a laugh
thrust it
            up into the animal's private parts.
                        I almost fainted.

Why should I think of that now?
            The cries of a dying dog
                        are to be blotted out
as best I can.
            René Char
                        you are a poet who believes
in the power of beauty
            to right all wrongs.
                        I believe it also.
With invention and courage
            we shall surpass
                        the pitiful dumb beasts,
let all men believe it,
            as you have taught me also
                        to believe it.

THE ARTIST

Mr. T.
            bareheaded
                        in a soiled undershirt
his hair standing out
            on all sides
                        stood on his toes
heels together
            arms gracefully
                        for the moment
curled above his head.
            Then he whirled about
                        bounded
into the air
            and with an *entrechat*
                        perfectly achieved
completed the figure.
            My mother
                        taken by surprise
where she sat
            in her invalid's chair
                        was left speechless.
Bravo! she cried at last
            and clapped her hands.
                        The man's wife
came from the kitchen:
            What goes on here? she said.
                        But the show was over.

A NEGRO WOMAN

carrying a bunch of marigolds
        wrapped
                in an old newspaper:
She carries them upright,
        bareheaded,
                the bulk
of her thighs
        causing her to waddle
                as she walks
looking into
        the store window which she passes
                on her way.
What is she
        but an ambassador
                from another world
a world of pretty marigolds
        of two shades
                which she announces
not knowing what she does
        other
                than walk the streets
holding the flowers upright
        as a torch
                so early in the morning.

THE PINK LOCUST

I'm persistent as the pink locust,
        once admitted
                to the garden,

you will not easily get rid of it.
            Tear it from the ground,
                        if one hair-thin rootlet
remain
            it will come again.
                        It is
flattering to think of myself
            so. It is also
                        laughable.
A modest flower,
            resembling a pink sweet-pea,
                        you cannot help
but admire it
            until its habits
                        become known.
Are we not most of us
            like that? It would be
                        too much
if the public
            pried among the minutiae
                        of our private affairs.
Not
            that we have anything to hide
                        but could *they*
stand it? Of course
            the world would be gratified
                        to find out
what fools we have made of ourselves.
            The question is,
                        would they
be generous with us —
            as we have been
                        with others? It is,

as I say,
           a flower
                     incredibly resilient
under attack!
           Neglect it
                     and it will grow into a tree.
I wish I could *so* think of myself
           and of what
                     is to become of me.
The poet himself,
           what does he think of himself
                     facing his world?
It will not do to say,
           as he is inclined to say:
                     Not much. The poem
would be in *that* betrayed.
           He might as well answer —
                     "a rose is a rose
is a rose" and let it go at that.
           A rose *is* a rose
                     and the poem equals it
if it be well made.
           The poet
                     cannot slight himself
without slighting
           his poem —
                     which would be
ridiculous.
           Life offers
                     no greater reward.
And so,
           like this flower,
                     I persist —

for what there may be in it.
          I am not,
                 I know,
in the galaxy of poets
          a rose
                but *who,* among the rest,
will deny me
          my place.

BIRD SONG

It is May on every hand
when the Towhee sings
to his silent mate

at the bottom of
the garden
flaunting his startling

colors moving restlessly
from one
leafless magnolia twig

to another —
announcing spring is
here spring is here

THE PARABLE OF THE BLIND

This horrible but superb painting
the parable of the blind
without a red

in the composition shows a group
of beggars leading
each other diagonally downward

across the canvas
from one side
to stumble finally into a bog

where the picture
and the composition ends back
of which no seeing man

is represented the unshaven
features of the des-
titute with their few

pitiful possessions a basin
to wash in a peasant
cottage is seen and a church spire

the faces are raised
as toward the light
there is no detail extraneous

to the composition one
follows the others stick in
hand triumphant to disaster

THE CHILDREN

Once in a while
we'd find a patch
of yellow violets

not many
but blue big blue
ones in

the cemetery woods
we'd pick
bunches of them

there was a family
named Foltette
a big family

with lots of
children's graves
so we'd take

bunches of violets
and place one
on each headstone

EXERCISE No. 2

The metal smokestack
of my neighbor's chimney
greets me among the new leaves

it is a small house
adjacent to my bigger one
I have come in 3 years

to know much of her
an old lady as I am an old man
we greet each other

across the hedge
my wife gives her flowers
we have never visited each other

SHORT POEM

You slapped my face
oh but so gently
I smiled
at the caress

To Flossie

who showed me
        a bunch of garden roses
she was keeping
        on ice

against an appointment
        with friends
for supper
        day after tomorrow

aren't they beautiful
        you can't
smell them
        because they're so cold

but aren't they
        in wax
paper for the
        moment beautiful

The Turtle

(For My Grandson)
Not because of his eyes,
        the eyes of a bird,
                but because he is beaked,
birdlike, to do an injury,
        has the turtle attracted you.
                He is your only pet.
When we are together
        you talk of nothing else
                ascribing all sorts

of murderous motives
             to his least action.
                          You ask me
to write a poem,
             should I have poems to write,
                          about a turtle.

The turtle lives in the mud
             but is not mud-like,
                          you can tell it by his eyes
which are clear.
             When he shall escape
                          his present confinement
he will stride about the world
             destroying all
                          with his sharp beak.
Whatever opposes him
             in the streets of the city
                          shall go down.
Cars will be overturned.
             And upon his back
                          shall ride,
to his conquests,
             my Lord,
                          you!
You shall be master!
             In the beginning
                          there was a great tortoise
who supported the world.
             Upon him
                          all ultimately
rests.

Without him
              nothing will stand.
He is all wise
          and can outrun the hare.
                    In the night
his eyes carry him
          to unknown places.
                    He is your friend.

ROBERT FROST

Robert Lee Frost, at least in his later years, was right out of central casting. With his shock of white hair, rough-hewn face, and wry New England manner, he played to perfection the role of benign homespun skeptic, winning over audiences at public readings from coast to coast. Asked once to explain a poem he had just recited, he retorted "What do you want me to do—say it over again in worser English?" Unquestionably our country's best-loved writer, he may not have been the kindest, gentlest man who ever lived (his official biographer suggests that behind the twinkling eyes lurked an egotistical tyrant), but he was certainly photogenic.

And dramatic. Nobody who watched John F. Kennedy's inauguration in 1961 is likely to forget the image of a weath-

ered old sage reading, in his inimitable voice, the patriotic
poem he selected for the occasion:

> The land was ours before we were the land's.
> She was our land more than a hundred years
> Before we were her people. She was ours
> In Massachusetts, in Virginia,
> But we were England's, still colonials,
> Possessing what we still were unpossessed by,
> Possessed by what we now no more possessed. . . .

"If you can bear at your age the honor of being made president
of the United States," he said to Kennedy, "I ought to be able
at my age to bear the honor of taking some part in your
inauguration." Eighty-six when he made his Washington ap-
pearance, Frost died two years later. The young president, who
was to be assassinated not long afterward, said, "He has be-
queathed his nation a body of imperishable verse from which
Americans will forever gain joy and understanding."

Whatever the poet's personal shortcomings, real or imag-
ined, he enjoyed a rare combination of popularity and critical
respectability, the latter indicated by no fewer than four Pu-
litzer Prizes, by two resolutions of praise from the U.S. Senate,
and by so many honorary degrees (the list includes Oxford and
Cambridge) that he had them sewn together to make a blanket.
Frost is to American poetry what Aaron Copland is to our
music; if anyone ever earned the right to be called our poet
laureate it was this cunning old Yankee whose "lover's quarrel
with the world" produced lines, alternatively playful and
tragic, that are etched in the minds of generations of citizens.

His climb to the top of Parnassus, however, was neither rapid nor easy, and it was not until he was nearly forty that the country began to take Frost to its heart. Born in San Francisco in 1874, he moved to Massachusetts with his mother, an amateur poet, eleven years later, following the death from tuberculosis of his alcoholic father, a newspaper reporter with a Harvard degree. Since his forebears for nine generations were New Englanders, the move, though traumatic for the boy, was something of a homecoming. After being graduated as valedictorian of his high school class, he attended Dartmouth College for a semester and then, as seems to be the way with budding writers, held a series of unrewarding jobs, including mill hand and newspaper reporter. He married a high school classmate after a difficult courtship that at one point took him to the verge of suicide. The young poet eventually enrolled as a special student at Harvard, where he stayed two years, studying Greek, Latin, and philosophy.

For the next decade Frost received what might be called a graduate education in the harsh realities of life, on a New Hampshire farm given to him, along with a small annuity, by his paternal grandfather. Failing miserably (he was a fine botanist but a terrible farmer), he helped make ends meet by teaching for a number of years. Then in 1911, at thirty-six, he sold the farm and moved with his wife and four young children to England, where the cost of living was comparatively low. Two years later his first book, *A Boy's Will,* composed of work he had written in New Hampshire, was published in England, followed the next year by *North of Boston,* narrative poems he called "a book of people." Both works were so well received by British critics that American publishers showed some interest; when he returned to his native soil in 1915 the poet, by now something of a celebrity, was wined, dined, and honored.

From the beginning, Frost's work showed the unmistakable stamp of the great British tradition he had all but committed to memory at an early age—Milton, Spenser, Keats, Shelley, and Browning, among others. Unimpressed by the compulsion of his fellow poets to "make it new," he was content, as he often said, with "old ways to be new." During the fifty years after his return from Europe he continued to publish his colloquial, craftily structured verse despite personal tragedies—a daughter went insane, another died during childbirth, and one of his sons committed suicide. He returned to farming, taught at Amherst and other colleges, and gradually developed what cultural historian Peter Conn calls "the artfully groomed benevolence of his public persona."

Frost had (and still has) a special appeal to harried city dwellers, who see in his orderly pastoral narratives, despite their unblinking focus on rural hardships and their frequently dark and even despairing sense of things, a vision of life rooted in permanent values and traditions far removed from the chaotic urban scene. His audience continues to be immense— if, in fact, there is anyone of a certain age who has never been exposed to "Stopping by Woods on a Snowy Evening," "The Road Not Taken," or "Birches," that individual has almost certainly been living in another galaxy.

All eleven of the poet's books are printed in *The Poetry of Robert Frost,* edited by Edward Connery Lathem (Henry

Holt, 1979). Lawrence Thompson is the author of a detailed and unflattering authorized biography: Volume 1, *Robert Frost: The Early Years, 1874–1915* (Rinehart and Winston, 1966); Volume 2, *Robert Frost: The Years of Triumph, 1915–1938,* (1970); and, with R. H. Winnick, Volume 3, *The Latter Years, 1938–1963* (1976). Two critical studies are especially recommended: Richard Poirier, *Robert Frost: The Work of Knowing* (Oxford University Press, 1977) and William H. Pritchard, *Frost: A Literary Life Reconsidered* (Oxford University Press, 1984).

THE PASTURE

I'm going out to clean the pasture spring;
I'll only stop to rake the leaves away
(And wait to watch the water clear, I may):
I shan't be gone long. — You come too.

I'm going out to fetch the little calf
That's standing by the mother. It's so young
It totters when she licks it with her tongue.
I shan't be gone long. — You come too.

MENDING WALL

Something there is that doesn't love a wall,
That sends the frozen-ground-swell under it
And spills the upper boulders in the sun,
And makes gaps even two can pass abreast.
The work of hunters is another thing:
I have come after them and made repair
Where they have left not one stone on a stone,

But they would have the rabbit out of hiding,
To please the yelping dogs. The gaps I mean,
No one has seen them made or heard them made,
But at spring mending-time we find them there.
I let my neighbor know beyond the hill;
And on a day we meet to walk the line
And set the wall between us once again.
We keep the wall between us as we go.
To each the boulders that have fallen to each.
And some are loaves and some so nearly balls
We have to use a spell to make them balance:
"Stay where you are until our backs are turned!"
We wear our fingers rough with handling them.
Oh, just another kind of outdoor game,
One on a side. It comes to little more:
There where it is we do not need the wall:
He is all pine and I am apple orchard.
My apple trees will never get across
And eat the cones under his pines, I tell him.
He only says, "Good fences make good neighbors."
Spring is the mischief in me, and I wonder
If I could put a notion in his head:
"*Why* do they make good neighbors? Isn't it
Where there are cows? But here there are no cows.
Before I built a wall I'd ask to know
What I was walling in or walling out,
And to whom I was like to give offense.
Something there is that doesn't love a wall,
That wants it down." I could say "Elves" to him,
But it's not elves exactly, and I'd rather
He said it for himself. I see him there,
Bringing a stone grasped firmly by the top
In each hand, like an old-stone savage armed.

He moves in darkness as it seems to me,
Not of woods only and the shade of trees.
He will not go behind his father's saying,
And he likes having thought of it so well
He says again, "Good fences make good neighbors."

THE DEATH OF THE HIRED MAN

Mary sat musing on the lamp-flame at the table,
Waiting for Warren. When she heard his step,
She ran on tiptoe down the darkened passage
To meet him in the doorway with the news
And put him on his guard. "Silas is back."
She pushed him outward with her through the door
And shut it after her. "Be kind," she said.
She took the market things from Warren's arms
And set them on the porch, then drew him down
To sit beside her on the wooden steps.

"When was I ever anything but kind to him?
But I'll not have the fellow back," he said.
"I told him so last haying, didn't I?
If he left then, I said, that ended it.
What good is he? Who else will harbor him
At his age for the little he can do?
What help he is there's no depending on.
Off he goes always when I need him most.
He thinks he ought to earn a little pay,
Enough at least to buy tobacco with,
So he won't have to beg and be beholden.
'All right,' I say, 'I can't afford to pay
Any fixed wages, though I wish I could.'
'Someone else can.' 'Then someone else will have to.'

I shouldn't mind his bettering himself
If that was what it was. You can be certain,
When he begins like that, there's someone at him
Trying to coax him off with pocket money —
In haying time, when any help is scarce.
In winter he comes back to us. I'm done."

"Sh! not so loud: he'll hear you," Mary said.

"I want him to: he'll have to soon or late."

"He's worn out. He's asleep beside the stove.
When I came up from Rowe's I found him here,
Huddled against the barn door fast asleep,
A miserable sight, and frightening, too —
You needn't smile — I didn't recognize him —
I wasn't looking for him — and he's changed.
Wait till you see."
                        "Where did you say he'd been?"
"He didn't say. I dragged him to the house,
And gave him tea and tried to make him smoke.
I tried to make him talk about his travels.
Nothing would do: he just kept nodding off."

"What did he say? Did he say anything?"

"But little."
                "Anything? Mary, confess
He said he'd come to ditch the meadow for me."

"Warren!"
            "But did he? I just want to know."

"Of course he did. What would you have him say?
Surely you wouldn't grudge the poor old man
Some humble way to save his self-respect.

He added, if you really care to know,
He meant to clear the upper pasture, too.
That sounds like something you have heard before?
Warren, I wish you could have heard the way
He jumbled everything. I stopped to look
Two or three times — he made me feel so queer —
To see if he was talking in his sleep.
He ran on Harold Wilson — you remember —
The boy you had in haying four years since.
He's finished school, and teaching in his college.
Silas declares you'll have to get him back.
He says they two will make a team for work:
Between them they will lay this farm as smooth!
The way he mixed that in with other things.
He thinks young Wilson a likely lad, though daft
On education — you know how they fought
All through July under the blazing sun,
Silas up on the cart to build the load,
Harold along beside to pitch it on."

"Yes, I took care to keep well out of earshot."

"Well, those days trouble Silas like a dream.
You wouldn't think they would. How some things linger!
Harold's young college-boy's assurance piqued him.
After so many years he still keeps finding
Good arguments he sees he might have used.
I sympathize. I know just how it feels
To think of the right thing to say too late.
Harold's associated in his mind with Latin.
He asked me what I thought of Harold's saying
He studied Latin, like the violin,
Because he liked it — that an argument!
He said he couldn't make the boy believe

He could find water with a hazel prong —
Which showed how much good school had ever done
    him.
He wanted to go over that. But most of all
He thinks if he could have another chance
To teach him how to build a load of hay — "

"I know, that's Silas' one accomplishment.
He bundles every forkful in its place,
And tags and numbers it for future reference,
So he can find and easily dislodge it
In the unloading. Silas does that well.
He takes it out in bunches like big birds' nests.
You never see him standing on the hay
He's trying to lift, straining to lift himself."

"He thinks if he could teach him that, he'd be
Some good perhaps to someone in the world.
He hates to see a boy the fool of books.
Poor Silas, so concerned for other folk,
And nothing to look backward to with pride,
And nothing to look forward to with hope,
So now and never any different."

Part of a moon was falling down the west,
Dragging the whole sky with it to the hills.
Its light poured softly in her lap. She saw it
And spread her apron to it. She put out her hand
Among the harplike morning-glory strings,
Taut with the dew from garden bed to eaves,
As if she played unheard some tenderness
That wrought on him beside her in the night.
"Warren," she said, "he has come home to die:
You needn't be afraid he'll leave you this time."

"Home," he mocked gently.

                           "Yes, what else but home?
It all depends on what you mean by home.
Of course he's nothing to us, any more
Than was the hound that came a stranger to us
Out of the woods, worn out upon the trail."

"Home is the place where, when you have to go there,
They have to take you in."

                         "I should have called it
Something you somehow haven't to deserve."

Warren leaned out and took a step or two,
Picked up a little stick, and brought it back
And broke it in his hand and tossed it by.
"Silas has better claim on us you think
Than on his brother? Thirteen little miles
As the road winds would bring him to his door.
Silas has walked that far no doubt today.
Why doesn't he go there? His brother's rich,
A somebody — director in the bank."

"He never told us that."

                         "We know it, though."

"I think his brother ought to help, of course.
I'll see to that if there is need. He ought of right
To take him in, and might be willing to —
He may be better than appearances.
But have some pity on Silas. Do you think
If he had any pride in claiming kin
Or anything he looked for from his brother,
He'd keep so still about him all this time?"

"I wonder what's between them."

                         "I can tell you.

Silas is what he is — we wouldn't mind him —
But just the kind that kinsfolk can't abide.
He never did a thing so very bad.
He don't know why he isn't quite as good
As anybody. Worthless though he is,
He won't be made ashamed to please his brother."

"*I* can't think Si ever hurt anyone."

"No, but he hurt my heart the way he lay
And rolled his old head on that sharp-edged chair-back.
He wouldn't let me put him on the lounge.
You must go in and see what you can do.
I made the bed up for him there tonight.
You'll be surprised at him — how much he's broken.
His working days are done; I'm sure of it."

"I'd not be in a hurry to say that."

"I haven't been. Go, look, see for yourself.
But, Warren, please remember how it is:
He's come to help you ditch the meadow.
He has a plan. You mustn't laugh at him.
He may not speak of it, and then he may.
I'll sit and see if that small sailing cloud
Will hit or miss the moon."
                                    It hit the moon.
Then there were three there, making a dim row,
The moon, the little silver cloud, and she.

Warren returned — too soon, it seemed to her —
Slipped to her side, caught up her hand and waited.

"Warren?" she questioned.
                              "Dead," was all he answered.

After Apple-Picking

My long two-pointed ladder's sticking through a tree
Toward heaven still,
And there's a barrel that I didn't fill
Beside it, and there may be two or three
Apples I didn't pick upon some bough.
But I am done with apple-picking now.
Essence of winter sleep is on the night,
The scent of apples: I am drowsing off.
I cannot rub the strangeness from my sight
I got from looking through a pane of glass
I skimmed this morning from the drinking trough
And held against the world of hoary grass.
It melted, and I let it fall and break.
But I was well
Upon my way to sleep before it fell,
And I could tell
What form my dreaming was about to take.
Magnified apples appear and disappear,
Stem end and blossom end,
And every fleck of russet showing clear.
My instep arch not only keeps the ache,
It keeps the pressure of a ladder-round.
I feel the ladder sway as the boughs bend.
And I keep hearing from the cellar bin
The rumbling sound
Of load on load of apples coming in.
For I have had too much
Of apple-picking: I am overtired
Of the great harvest I myself desired.
There were ten thousand thousand fruit to touch,
Cherish in hand, lift down, and not let fall.

For all
That struck the earth,
No matter if not bruised or spiked with stubble,
Went surely to the cider-apple heap
As of no worth.
One can see what will trouble
This sleep of mine, whatever sleep it is.
Were he not gone,
The woodchuck could say whether it's like his
Long sleep, as I describe its coming on,
Or just some human sleep.

THE WOOD-PILE

Out walking in the frozen swamp one gray day,
I paused and said, "I will turn back from here.
No, I will go on farther — and we shall see."
The hard snow held me, save where now and then
One foot went through. The view was all in lines
Straight up and down of tall slim trees
Too much alike to mark or name a place by
So as to say for certain I was here
Or somewhere else: I was just far from home.
A small bird flew before me. He was careful
To put a tree between us when he lighted,
And say no word to tell me who he was
Who was so foolish as to think what *he* thought.
He thought that I was after him for a feather —
The white one in his tail; like one who takes
Everything said as personal to himself.
One flight out sideways would have undeceived him.
And then there was a pile of wood for which
I forgot him and let his little fear

Carry him off the way I might have gone,
Without so much as wishing him good-night.
He went behind it to make his last stand.
It was a cord of maple, cut and split
And piled — and measured, four by four by eight.
And not another like it could I see.
No runner tracks in this year's snow looped near it.
And it was older sure than this year's cutting,
Or even last year's or the year's before.
The wood was gray and the bark warping off it
And the pile somewhat sunken. Clematis
Had wound strings round and round it like a bundle.
What held it, though, on one side was a tree
Still growing, and on one a stake and prop,
These latter about to fall. I thought that only
Someone who lived in turning to fresh tasks
Could so forget his handiwork on which
He spent himself, the labor of his ax,
And leave it there far from a useful fireplace
To warm the frozen swamp as best it could
With the slow smokeless burning of decay.

THE ROAD NOT TAKEN

Two roads diverged in a yellow wood,
And sorry I could not travel both
And be one traveler, long I stood
And looked down one as far as I could
To where it bent in the undergrowth;

Then took the other, as just as fair,
And having perhaps the better claim,
Because it was grassy and wanted wear;

Though as for that, the passing there
Had worn them really about the same,

And both that morning equally lay
In leaves no step had trodden black.
Oh, I kept the first for another day!
Yet knowing how way leads on to way,
I doubted if I should ever come back.

I shall be telling this with a sigh
Somewhere ages and ages hence:
Two roads diverged in a wood, and I —
I took the one less traveled by,
And that has made all the difference.

BIRCHES

When I see birches bend to left and right
Across the lines of straighter darker trees,
I like to think some boy's been swinging them.
But swinging doesn't bend them down to stay
As ice storms do. Often you must have seen them
Loaded with ice a sunny winter morning
After a rain. They click upon themselves
As the breeze rises, and turn many-colored
As the stir cracks and crazes their enamel.
Soon the sun's warmth makes them shed crystal shells
Shattering and avalanching on the snow crust —
Such heaps of broken glass to sweep away
You'd think the inner dome of heaven had fallen.
They are dragged to the withered bracken by the load,
And they seem not to break; though once they are bowed
So low for long, they never right themselves:
You may see their trunks arching in the woods

Years afterwards, trailing their leaves on the ground
Like girls on hands and knees that throw their hair
Before them over their heads to dry in the sun.
But I was going to say when Truth broke in
With all her matter of fact about the ice storm,
I should prefer to have some boy bend them
As he went out and in to fetch the cows —
Some boy too far from town to learn baseball,
Whose only play was what he found himself,
Summer or winter, and could play alone.
One by one he subdued his father's trees
By riding them down over and over again
Until he took the stiffness out of them,
And not one but hung limp, not one was left
For him to conquer. He learned all there was
To learn about not launching out too soon
And so not carrying the tree away
Clear to the ground. He always kept his poise
To the top branches, climbing carefully
With the same pains you use to fill a cup
Up to the brim, and even above the brim.
Then he flung outward, feet first, with a swish,
Kicking his way down through the air to the ground.
So was I once myself a swinger of birches.
And so I dream of going back to be.
It's when I'm weary of considerations,
And life is too much like a pathless wood
Where your face burns and tickles with the cobwebs
Broken across it, and one eye is weeping
From a twig's having lashed across it open.
I'd like to get away from earth awhile
And then come back to it and begin over.
May no fate willfully misunderstand me

And half grant what I wish and snatch me away
Not to return. Earth's the right place for love:
I don't know where it's likely to go better.
I'd like to go by climbing a birch tree,
And climb black branches up a snow-white trunk
Toward heaven, till the tree could bear no more,
But dipped its top and set me down again.
That would be good both going and coming back.
One could do worse than be a swinger of birches.

FIRE AND ICE

Some say the world will end in fire,
Some say in ice.
From what I've tasted of desire
I hold with those who favor fire.
But if it had to perish twice,
I think I know enough of hate
To say that for destruction ice
Is also great
And would suffice.

DUST OF SNOW

The way a crow
Shook down on me
The dust of snow
From a hemlock tree

Has given my heart
A change of mood
And saved some part
Of a day I had rued.

THE RUNAWAY

Once when the snow of the year was beginning to fall,
We stopped by a mountain pasture to say, "Whose colt?"
A little Morgan had one forefoot on the wall,
The other curled at his breast. He dipped his head
And snorted at us. And then he had to bolt.
We heard the miniature thunder where he fled,
And we saw him, or thought we saw him, dim and gray,
Like a shadow against the curtain of falling flakes.
"I think the little fellow's afraid of the snow.
He isn't winter-broken. It isn't play
With the little fellow at all. He's running away.
I doubt if even his mother could tell him, 'Sakes,
It's only weather.' He'd think she didn't know!
Where is his mother? He can't be out alone."
And now he comes again with clatter of stone,
And mounts the wall again with whited eyes
And all his tail that isn't hair up straight.
He shudders his coat as if to throw off flies.
"Whoever it is that leaves him out so late,
When other creatures have gone to stall and bin,
Ought to be told to come and take him in."

STOPPING BY WOODS
ON A SNOWY EVENING

Whose woods these are I think I know.
His house is in the village, though;
He will not see me stopping here
To watch his woods fill up with snow.

My little horse must think it queer
To stop without a farmhouse near
Between the woods and frozen lake
The darkest evening of the year.

He gives his harness bells a shake
To ask if there is some mistake.
The only other sound's the sweep
Of easy wind and downy flake.

The woods are lovely, dark, and deep,
But I have promises to keep,
And miles to go before I sleep,
And miles to go before I sleep.

THE NEED OF BEING VERSED
IN COUNTRY THINGS

The house had gone to bring again
To the midnight sky a sunset glow.
Now the chimney was all of the house that stood,
Like a pistil after the petals go.

The barn opposed across the way,
That would have joined the house in flame
Had it been the will of the wind, was left
To bear forsaken the place's name.

No more it opened with all one end
For teams that came by the stony road
To drum on the floor with scurrying hoofs
And brush the mow with the summer load.

The birds that came to it through the air
At broken windows flew out and in,

Their murmur more like the sigh we sigh
From too much dwelling on what has been.

Yet for them the lilac renewed its leaf,
And the aged elm, though touched with fire;
And the dry pump flung up an awkward arm;
And the fence post carried a strand of wire.

For them there was really nothing sad.
But though they rejoiced in the nest they kept,
One had to be versed in country things
Not to believe the phoebes wept.

FIREFLIES IN THE GARDEN

Here come real stars to fill the upper skies,
And here on earth come emulating flies
That, though they never equal stars in size
(And they were never really stars at heart),
Achieve at times a very starlike start.
Only, of course, they can't sustain the part.

A MINOR BIRD

I have wished a bird would fly away,
And not sing by my house all day;

Have clapped my hands at him from the door
When it seemed as if I could bear no more.

The fault must partly have been in me.
The bird was not to blame for his key.

And of course there must be something wrong
In wanting to silence any song.

ACQUAINTED WITH THE NIGHT

I have been one acquainted with the night.
I have walked out in rain — and back in rain.
I have outwalked the furthest city light.

I have looked down the saddest city lane.
I have passed by the watchman on his beat
And dropped my eyes, unwilling to explain.

I have stood still and stopped the sound of feet
When far away an interrupted cry
Came over houses from another street,

But not to call me back or say good-by;
And further still at an unearthly height
One luminary clock against the sky

Proclaimed the time was neither wrong nor right.
I have been one acquainted with the night.

TWO TRAMPS IN MUD TIME

Out of the mud two strangers came
And caught me splitting wood in the yard.
And one of them put me off my aim
By hailing cheerily "Hit them hard!"
I knew pretty well why he dropped behind
And let the other go on a way.
I knew pretty well what he had in mind:
He wanted to take my job for pay.

Good blocks of oak it was I split,
As large around as the chopping block;
And every piece I squarely hit

Fell splinterless as a cloven rock.
The blows that a life of self-control
Spares to strike for the common good,
That day, giving a loose to my soul,
I spent on the unimportant wood.

The sun was warm but the wind was chill.
You know how it is with an April day
When the sun is out and the wind is still,
You're one month on in the middle of May.
But if you so much as dare to speak,
A cloud comes over the sunlit arch,
A wind comes off a frozen peak,
And you're two months back in the middle of March.

A bluebird comes tenderly up to alight
And turns to the wind to unruffle a plume,
His song so pitched as not to excite
A single flower as yet to bloom.
It is snowing a flake: and he half knew
Winter was only playing possum.
Except in color he isn't blue,
But he wouldn't advise a thing to blossom.

The water for which we may have to look
In summertime with a witching wand,
In every wheelrut's now a brook,
In every print of a hoof a pond.
Be glad of water, but don't forget
The lurking frost in the earth beneath
That will steal forth after the sun is set
And show on the water its crystal teeth.

The time when most I loved my task
These two must make me love it more

By coming with what they came to ask.
You'd think I never had felt before
The weight of an ax-head poised aloft,
The grip on earth of outspread feet,
The life of muscles rocking soft
And smooth and moist in vernal heat.

Out of the woods two hulking tramps
(From sleeping God knows where last night,
But not long since in the lumber camps).
They thought all chopping was theirs of right.
Men of the woods and lumberjacks,
They judged me by their appropriate tool.
Except as a fellow handled an ax
They had no way of knowing a fool.

Nothing on either side was said.
They knew they had but to stay their stay
And all their logic would fill my head:
As that I had no right to play
With what was another man's work for gain.
My right might be love but theirs was need.
And where the two exist in twain
Theirs was the better right — agreed.

But yield who will to their separation,
My object in living is to unite
My avocation and my vocation
As my two eyes make one in sight.
Only where love and need are one,
And the work is play for mortal stakes,
Is the deed ever really done
For Heaven and the future's sakes.

DESIGN

I found a dimpled spider, fat and white,
On a white heal-all, holding up a moth
Like a white piece of rigid satin cloth —
Assorted characters of death and blight
Mixed ready to begin the morning right,
Like the ingredients of a witches' broth —
A snow-drop spider, a flower like a froth,
And dead wings carried like a paper kite.

What had that flower to do with being white,
The wayside blue and innocent heal-all?
What brought the kindred spider to that height,
Then steered the white moth thither in the night?
What but design of darkness to appall? —
If design govern in a thing so small.

UNHARVESTED

A scent of ripeness from over a wall.
And come to leave the routine road
And look for what had made me stall,
There sure enough was an apple tree
That had eased itself of its summer load,
And of all but its trivial foliage free,
Now breathed as light as a lady's fan.
For there there had been an apple fall
As complete as the apple had given man.
The ground was one circle of solid red.

May something go always unharvested!
May much stay out of our stated plan,
Apples or something forgotten and left,
So smelling their sweetness would be no theft.

THE BEARER OF EVIL TIDINGS

The bearer of evil tidings,
When he was halfway there,
Remembered that evil tidings
Were a dangerous thing to bear.

So when he came to the parting
Where one road led to the throne
And one went off to the mountains
And into the wild unknown,

He took the one to the mountains.
He ran through the Vale of Cashmere,
He ran through the rhododendrons
Till he came to the land of Pamir.

And there in a precipice valley
A girl of his age he met
Took him home to her bower,
Or he might be running yet.

She taught him her tribe's religion:
How, ages and ages since,
A princess en route from China
To marry a Persian prince

Had been found with child; and her army
Had come to a troubled halt.
And though a god was the father
And nobody else at fault,

It had seemed discreet to remain there
And neither go on nor back.
So they stayed and declared a village
There in the land of the Yak.

And the child that came of the princess
Established a royal line,
And his mandates were given heed to
Because he was born divine.

And that was why there were people
On one Himalayan shelf;
And the bearer of evil tidings
Decided to stay there himself.

At least he had this in common
With the race he chose to adopt:
They had both of them had their reasons
For stopping where they had stopped.

As for his evil tidings,
Belshazzar's overthrow,
Why hurry to tell Belshazzar
What soon enough he would know?

A CONSIDERABLE SPECK

(Microscopic)
A speck that would have been beneath my sight
On any but a paper sheet so white
Set off across what I had written there.
And I had idly poised my pen in air
To stop it with a period of ink,
When something strange about it made me think.
This was no dust speck by my breathing blown,

But unmistakably a living mite
With inclinations it could call its own.
It paused as with suspicion of my pen,
And then came racing wildly on again
To where my manuscript was not yet dry;
Then paused again and either drank or smelt —
With loathing, for again it turned to fly.
Plainly with an intelligence I dealt.
It seemed too tiny to have room for feet,
Yet must have had a set of them complete
To express how much it didn't want to die.
It ran with terror and with cunning crept.
It faltered: I could see it hesitate;
Then in the middle of the open sheet
Cower down in desperation to accept
Whatever I accorded it of fate.
I have none of the tenderer-than-thou
Collectivistic regimenting love
With which the modern world is being swept.
But this poor microscopic item now!
Since it was nothing I knew evil of
I let it lie there till I hope it slept.

I have a mind myself and recognize
Mind when I meet with it in any guise.
No one can know how glad I am to find
On any sheet the least display of mind.

A YOUNG BIRCH

The birch begins to crack its outer sheath
Of baby green and show the white beneath,
As whosoever likes the young and slight

May well have noticed. Soon entirely white
To double day and cut in half the dark
It will stand forth, entirely white in bark,
And nothing but the top a leafy green —
The only native tree that dares to lean,
Relying on its beauty, to the air.
(Less brave perhaps than trusting are the fair.)
And someone reminiscent will recall
How once in cutting brush along the wall
He spared it from the number of the slain,
At first to be no bigger than a cane,
And then no bigger than a fishing pole,
But now at last so obvious a bole
The most efficient help you ever hired
Would know that it was there to be admired,
And zeal would not be thanked that cut it down
When you were reading books or out of town.
It was a thing of beauty and was sent
To live its life out as an ornament.

DIRECTIVE

Back out of all this now too much for us,
Back in a time made simple by the loss
Of detail, burned, dissolved, and broken off
Like graveyard marble sculpture in the weather,
There is a house that is no more a house
Upon a farm that is no more a farm
And in a town that is no more a town.
The road there, if you'll let a guide direct you
Who only has at heart your getting lost,
May seem as if it should have been a quarry —

Great monolithic knees the former town
Long since gave up pretense of keeping covered.
And there's a story in a book about it:
Besides the wear of iron wagon wheels
The ledges show lines ruled southeast-northwest,
The chisel work of an enormous Glacier
That braced his feet against the Arctic Pole.
You must not mind a certain coolness from him
Still said to haunt this side of Panther Mountain.
Nor need you mind the serial ordeal
Of being watched from forty cellar holes
As if by eye pairs out of forty firkins.
As for the woods' excitement over you
That sends light rustle rushes to their leaves,
Charge that to upstart inexperience.
Where were they all not twenty years ago?
They think too much of having shaded out
A few old pecker-fretted apple trees.
Make yourself up a cheering song of how
Someone's road home from work this once was,
Who may be just ahead of you on foot
Or creaking with a buggy load of grain.
The height of the adventure is the height
Of country where two village cultures faded
Into each other. Both of them are lost.
And if you're lost enough to find yourself
By now, pull in your ladder road behind you
And put a sign up CLOSED to all but me.
Then make yourself at home. The only field
Now left's no bigger than a harness gall.
First there's the children's house of make-believe,
Some shattered dishes underneath a pine,
The playthings in the playhouse of the children.

Weep for what little things could make them glad.
Then for the house that is no more a house,
But only a belilaced cellar hole,
Now slowly closing like a dent in dough.
This was no playhouse but a house in earnest.
Your destination and your destiny's
A brook that was the water of the house,
Cold as a spring as yet so near its source,
Too lofty and original to rage.
(We know the valley streams that when aroused
Will leave their tatters hung on barb and thorn.)
I have kept hidden in the instep arch
Of an old cedar at the waterside
A broken drinking goblet like the Grail
Under a spell so the wrong ones can't find it,
So can't get saved, as Saint Mark says they mustn't.
(I stole the goblet from the children's playhouse.)
Here are your waters and your watering place.
Drink and be whole again beyond confusion.

[Forgive, O Lord . . .]

Forgive, O Lord, my little jokes on Thee
And I'll forgive Thy great big one on me.

The Draft Horse

With a lantern that wouldn't burn
In too frail a buggy we drove
Behind too heavy a horse
Through a pitch-dark limitless grove.

And a man came out of the trees
And took our horse by the head
And reaching back to his ribs
Deliberately stabbed him dead.

The ponderous beast went down
With a crack of a broken shaft.
And the night drew through the trees
In one long invidious draft.

The most unquestioning pair
That ever accepted fate
And the least disposed to ascribe
Any more than we had to to hate,

We assumed that the man himself
Or someone he had to obey
Wanted us to get down
And walk the rest of the way.

LANGSTON HUGHES

Like Whitman, one of his heroes, James Mercer Langston Hughes, born in Missouri in 1902, called a number of places home during his childhood. Unlike his great predecessor, however, he did not have the benefit of a stable family life to provide a sense of emotional security. The boy's stagestruck mother was frequently absent, and his ill-tempered father (whom he hated), a man with undisguised disdain for most other blacks, moved to Mexico to escape American oppression. It was left to the boy's poor but self-reliant grandmother to raise him, and thus he spent many of his formative years in Lawrence, Kansas. After her death, he lived with his mother in several cities before they settled in Cleveland. "My theory is," he later wrote, "children should be born without parents—if born they must be."

It is nowhere carved in stone that an unhappy childhood is a requisite for artistic development, but his own early misfortunes clearly had some advantages for young Langston: he not only developed a rich fantasy life as an alternative to a lonely reality (his color kept him out of the Boy Scouts, the YMCA, and movie theaters) but discovered the solace and redeeming power of books. From an early age he read deeply—Whitman, Longfellow, Vachel Lindsay, and Carl Sandburg (his "guiding star"), and also W. E. B. Du Bois (*The Souls of Black Folk*) and, especially, Paul Laurence Dunbar, who wrote in black dialect. By the time the intellectually gifted young man had reached his late teens he had already begun to publish the poems that would make him "Poet Laureate of the Negro Race" (a title he may have given himself). Arnold Rampersad, his biographer, tells us that it was not until years later that "the blues" orchestrated his private melancholy and gave it form, but the poet was clearly on his way.

After a year at Columbia University, where he was the only black student living on campus, he held a series of odd jobs and then traveled in Africa, France, and Italy. While his ship was steaming out of New York bound for Africa, the twenty-two-year-old poet suddenly threw overboard the books he had packed, thus symbolically unburdening himself of his past. He saved only his copy of *Leaves of Grass*: "I had no intention of throwing that one away." Returning to the States, he worked in a restaurant, and one day put three of his poems beside Vachel Lindsay's plate. The famous poet announced at a public reading that he had discovered a busboy poet, and newspapers covered the story. Partly as a result, Hughes received a scholarship to Lincoln University in Pennsylvania (one of his classmates was Thurgood Marshall), and during his years there he published *The Weary Blues,* the first of his more than forty books. This volume was followed a year later by *Fine Clothes to the Jew,* which scandalized some black reviewers, who feared that its focus on the bleaker aspects of life, coupled with the use of dialect, would play into the hands of a hostile white world.

In basing his poetry on the blues, the young writer wanted to create works of art that all his people would understand; as Rampersad says, he "fashioned an aesthetic of simplicity born out of the speech, music, and actual social conditions of his people." Hughes is, along with Williams and Frost, among the more accessible of modern American poets; in their work, clarity results not from intellectual poverty but from judicious artistic choices. These poets reinforce Randall Jarrell's assertion that those who have inherited the custom of not reading poetry justify it by referring to the obscurity of the poems they have never read.

In addition to his numerous books of verse, Hughes composed a novel, short stories, essays, film scripts, plays, opera librettos, and an autobiography. The exuberant play *Mule Bone,* which he wrote with Zora Neale Hurston, was finally produced by New York City's Lincoln Center in 1991. He also edited anthologies of black poetry and folklore. No matter what the genre, his subject was nearly always the same: the experience of being black in the United States. In recognition of his impressive body of work he was named a Guggenheim Foundation Fellow in 1936 and also received a grant from the American Academy of Arts and Letters, a prestigious honor society of leading artists that later elected him to its membership.

Radical in his younger years ("Put one more 'S' in the USA / and make it Soviet"), he traveled widely in Russia, Japan, and Haiti, and covered the Spanish Civil War in 1937 as a newspaper correspondent. As he grew older his views became increasingly noncontroversial. A central figure in the period of intense productivity of African American art during the twenties and thirties known as the Harlem Renaissance, he had a powerful impact on many young black poets, who followed his lead in drawing on the tradition of the blues.

Curiously, despite his generosity of spirit and likable disposition (including an extraordinary gift for laughter), there is no evidence that Hughes formed any intense and lasting emotional ties: behind the warm smile, Arthur Koestler wrote, "one felt an impenetrable, elusive remoteness which warded off all undue familiarity." It is surprising, too, given his productivity and influence, that he never achieved financial security but had to continue throughout his life earning his way with his pen. He died at sixty-five in New York, having left instructions for his mourners to dress in red, "Cause there ain't no sense / In my being dead." At his memorial service a pianist played Duke Ellington's "Do Nothin' Till You Hear from Me," one of the poet's favorite songs. Twenty-four years later, in 1991, his ashes were interred beneath the floor of an auditorium named in his honor at the Schomburg Center for Research in Black Culture in his beloved Harlem, the "great dark city."

Selected Poems of Langston Hughes (Vintage Books, 1974). For biographical information, see Arnold Rampersad, *The Life of Langston Hughes*. Volume 1: *I, Too, Sing America* (Oxford University Press, 1986); Volume 2: *1941–1967, I Dream a World*

(1988); and *The Big Sea, An Autobiography* (Alfred A. Knopf, 1940). See also Jemie Onwuchekwa, *Langston Hughes: An Introduction to the Poetry* (Columbia University Press, 1977).

AUNT SUE'S STORIES

Aunt Sue has a head full of stories.
Aunt Sue has a whole heart full of stories.
Summer nights on the front porch
Aunt Sue cuddles a brown-faced child to her bosom
And tells him stories.

Black slaves
Working in the hot sun,
And black slaves
Walking in the dewy night,
And black slaves
Singing sorrow songs on the banks of a mighty river
Mingle themselves softly
In the flow of old Aunt Sue's voice,
Mingle themselves softly
In the dark shadows that cross and recross
Aunt Sue's stories.

And the dark-faced child, listening,
Knows that Aunt Sue's stories are real stories.
He knows that Aunt Sue never got her stories
Out of any book at all,
But that they came
Right out of her own life.

The dark-faced child is quiet
Of a summer night
Listening to Aunt Sue's stories.

Dream Variations

To fling my arms wide
In some place of the sun,
To whirl and to dance
Till the white day is done.
Then rest at cool evening
Beneath a tall tree
While night comes on gently,
    Dark like me —
That is my dream!

To fling my arms wide
In the face of the sun,
Dance! Whirl! Whirl!
Till the quick day is done.
Rest at pale evening . . .
A tall, slim tree . . .
Night coming tenderly
    Black like me.

Tambourines

Tambourines!
Tambourines!
Tambourines
To the glory of God!
Tambourines
To glory!

A gospel shout
And a gospel song:

Life is short
But God is long!

Tambourines!
Tambourines!
Tambourines
To glory!

THE WEARY BLUES

Droning a drowsy syncopated tune,
Rocking back and forth to a mellow croon,
    I heard a Negro play.
Down on Lenox Avenue the other night
By the pale dull pallor of an old gas light
    He did a lazy sway. . . .
    He did a lazy sway. . . .
To the tune o' those Weary Blues.
With his ebony hands on each ivory key
He made that poor piano moan with melody.
    O Blues!
Swaying to and fro on his rickety stool
He played that sad raggy tune like a musical fool.
    Sweet Blues!
Coming from a black man's soul.
    O Blues!
In a deep song voice with a melancholy tone
I heard that Negro sing, that old piano moan —
    "Ain't got nobody in all this world,
    Ain't got nobody but ma self.
    I's gwine to quit ma frownin'
    And put ma troubles on the shelf."

Thump, thump, thump, went his foot on the floor.
He played a few chords then he sang some more —
    "I got the Weary Blues
    And I can't be satisfied.
    Got the Weary Blues
    And can't be satisfied —
    I ain't happy no mo'
    And I wish that I had died."
And far into the night he crooned that tune.
The stars went out and so did the moon.
The singer stopped playing and went to bed
While the Weary Blues echoed through his head.
He slept like a rock or a man that's dead.

SYLVESTER'S DYING BED

I woke up this mornin'
'Bout half-past three.
All the womens in town
Was gathered round me.

Sweet gals was a-moanin',
"Sylvester's gonna die!"
And a hundred pretty mamas
Bowed their heads to cry.

I woke up little later
'Bout half-past fo',
The doctor 'n' undertaker's
Both at ma do'.

Black gals was a-beggin',
"You can't leave us here!"

Brown-skins cryin', "Daddy!
Honey! Baby! Don't go, dear!"

But I felt ma time's a-comin',
And I know'd I's dyin' fast.
I seed the River Jerden
A-creepin' muddy past —
But I's still Sweet Papa 'Vester,
Yes, sir! Long as life do last!

So I hollers, "Com'ere, babies,
Fo' to love yo' daddy right!"
And I reaches up to hug 'em —
When the Lawd put out the light.

Then everything was darkness
In a great . . . big . . . night.

BAD LUCK CARD

Cause you don't love me
Is awful, awful hard.
Gypsy done showed me
My bad luck card.

There ain't no good left
In this world for me.
Gypsy done tole me —
Unlucky as can be.

I don't know what
Po' weary me can do.
Gypsy says I'd kill my self
If I was you.

EARLY EVENING QUARREL

Where is that sugar, Hammond,
I sent you this morning to buy?
I say, where is that sugar
I sent you this morning to buy?
Coffee without sugar
Makes a good woman cry.

> *I ain't got no sugar, Hattie,*
> *I gambled your dime away.*
> *Ain't got no sugar, I*
> *Done gambled that dime away.*
> *If you's a wise woman, Hattie,*
> *You ain't gonna have nothin to say.*

I ain't no wise woman, Hammond.
I am evil and mad.
Ain't no sense in a good woman
Bein treated so bad.

> *I don't treat you bad, Hattie,*
> *Neither does I treat you good.*
> *But I reckon I could treat you*
> *Worser if I would.*

Lawd, these things we women
Have to stand!
I wonder is there nowhere a
Do-right man?

WATER-FRONT STREETS

The spring is not so beautiful there —
　　But dream ships sail away
To where the spring is wondrous rare
　　And life is gay.

The spring is not so beautiful there —
　　But lads put out to sea
Who carry beauties in their hearts
　　And dreams, like me.

IN TIME OF SILVER RAIN

In time of silver rain
The earth
Puts forth new life again,
Green grasses grow
And flowers lift their heads,
And over all the plain
The wonder spreads
　　Of life,
　　Of life,
　　Of life!

In time of silver rain
The butterflies
Lift silken wings
To catch a rainbow cry,
And trees put forth
New leaves to sing

In joy beneath the sky
As down the roadway
Passing boys and girls
Go singing, too,
In time of silver rain
When spring
And life
Are new.

WINTER MOON

How thin and sharp is the moon tonight!
How thin and sharp and ghostly white
Is the slim curved crook of the moon tonight!

SUICIDE'S NOTE

The calm,
Cool face of the river
Asked me for a kiss.

VAGABONDS

We are the desperate
Who do not care,
The hungry
Who have nowhere
To eat,
No place to sleep,
The tearless
Who cannot
Weep.

LUCK

Sometimes a crumb falls
From the tables of joy,
Sometimes a bone
Is flung.

To some people
Love is given,
To others
Only heaven.

LOVER'S RETURN

My old time daddy
Came back home last night.
His face was pale and
His eyes didn't look just right.

He says, "Mary, I'm
Comin' home to you —
So sick and lonesome
I don't know what to do."

Oh, men treats women
Just like a pair o' shoes —
You kicks 'em round and
Does 'em like you choose.

I looked at my daddy —
Lawd! and I wanted to cry.
He looked so thin —
Lawd! that I wanted to cry.
But the devil told me:
Damn a lover
Come home to die!

MISS BLUES'ES CHILD

If the blues would let me,
Lord knows I would smile.
If the blues would let me,
I would smile, smile, smile.
Instead of that I'm cryin' —
I must be Miss Blues'es child.

You were my moon up in the sky,
At night my wishing star.
I love you, oh, I love you so —
But you have gone so far!

Now my days are lonely,
And night-time drives me wild.
In my heart I'm crying,
I'm just Miss Blues'es child!

STONY LONESOME

They done took Cordelia
Out to stony lonesome ground.
Done took Cordelia
To stony lonesome,
Laid her down.
They done put Cordelia
Underneath that
Grassless mound.
Ay-Lord!
Ay-Lord!
Ay-Lord!

She done left po' Buddy
To struggle by his self.
Po' Buddy Jones,
Yes, he's done been left.
She's out in stony lonesome,
Lordy! Sleepin' by herself.
    Cordelia's
      In stony
        Lonesome
          Ground!

LIFE IS FINE

I went down to the river,
I set down on the bank.
I tried to think but couldn't,
So I jumped in and sank.

I came up once and hollered!
I came up twice and cried!
If that water hadn't a-been so cold
I might've sunk and died.

    But it was
    Cold in that water!
    It was cold!

I took the elevator
Sixteen floors above the ground.
I thought about my baby
And thought I would jump down.

I stood there and I hollered!
I stood there and I cried!

If it hadn't a-been so high
I might've jumped and died.

    But it was
    High up there!
    It was high!

So since I'm still here livin',
I guess I will live on.
I could've died for love —
But for livin' I was born.

Though you may hear me holler,
And you may see me cry —
I'll be dogged, sweet baby,
If you gonna see me die.

    Life is fine!
    Fine as wine!
    Life is fine!

STILL HERE

I've been scarred and battered.
My hopes the wind done scattered.
Snow has friz me, sun has baked me.
    Looks like between 'em
    They done tried to make me
Stop laughin', stop lovin', stop livin' —
    But I don't care!
    I'm still here!

Blue Monday

No use in my going
Downtown to work today,
    It's eight,
    I'm late —
And it's marked down that-a-way.

Saturday and Sunday's
Fun to sport around.
But no use denying —
Monday'll get you down.

That old blue Monday
Will surely get you down.

Homecoming

I went back in the alley
And I opened up my door.
All her clothes was gone:
She wasn't home no more.

I pulled back the covers,
I made down the bed.
A *whole* lot of room
Was the only thing I had.

Ballad of the Girl Whose Name Is Mud

A girl with all that raising,
It's hard to understand
How she could get in trouble
With a no-good man.

The guy she gave her all to
Dropped her with a thud.
Now amongst decent people,
Dorothy's name is mud.

But nobody's seen her shed a tear,
Nor seen her hang her head.
Ain't even heard her murmur,
Lord, I wish I was dead!

No! The hussy's telling everybody —
Just as though it was no sin —
That if she had a chance
She'd do it agin'!

LITTLE OLD LETTER

It was yesterday morning
I looked in my box for mail.
The letter that I found there
Made me turn right pale.

Just a little old letter,
Wasn't even one page long —
But it made me wish
I was in my grave and gone.

I turned it over,
Not a word writ on the back.
I never felt so lonesome
Since I was born black.

Just a pencil and paper,
You don't need no gun nor knife —
A little old letter
Can take a person's life.

CROSS

My old man's a white old man
And my old mother's black.
If ever I cursed my white old man
I take my curses back.

If ever I cursed my black old mother
And wished she were in hell,
I'm sorry for that evil wish
And now I wish her well.

My old man died in a fine big house.
My ma died in a shack.
I wonder where I'm gonna die,
Being neither white nor black?

SHARE-CROPPERS

Just a herd of Negroes
Driven to the field,
Plowing, planting, hoeing,
To make the cotton yield.

When the cotton's picked
And the work is done
Boss man takes the money
And we get none,

Leaves us hungry, ragged
As we were before.
Year by year goes by
And we are nothing more

Than a herd of Negroes
Driven to the field —
Plowing life away
To make the cotton yield.

UNCLE TOM

Within —
The beaten pride.
Without —
The grinning face,
The low, obsequious,
Double bow,
The sly and servile grace
Of one the white folks
Long ago
Taught well
To know his
Place.

SONG FOR A DARK GIRL

Way Down South in Dixie
    (Break the heart of me)
They hung my black young lover
    To a cross roads tree.

Way Down South in Dixie
    (Bruised body high in air)
I asked the white Lord Jesus
    What was the use of prayer.

Way Down South in Dixie
   (Break the heart of me)
Love is a naked shadow
   On a gnarled and naked tree.

MOTHER TO SON

Well, son, I'll tell you:
Life for me ain't been no crystal stair.
It's had tacks in it,
And splinters,
And boards torn up,
And places with no carpet on the floor —
Bare.
But all the time
I'se been a-climbin' on,
And reachin' landin's,
And turnin' corners,
And sometimes goin' in the dark
Where there ain't been no light.
So boy, don't you turn back.
Don't you set down on the steps
'Cause you finds it's kinder hard.
Don't you fall now —
For I'se still goin', honey,
I'se still climbin',
And life for me ain't been no crystal stair.

MERRY-GO-ROUND

Colored child at carnival:
Where is the Jim Crow section
On this merry-go-round,

Mister, cause I want to ride?
Down South where I come from
White and colored
Can't sit side by side.
Down South on the train
There's a Jim Crow car.
On the bus we're put in the back —
But there ain't no back
To a merry-go-round!
Where's the horse
For a kid that's black?

BALLAD OF THE MAN WHO'S GONE

No money to bury him.
The relief gave Forty-Four.
The undertaker told 'em,
You'll need Sixty more

For a first-class funeral,
A hearse and two cars —
And maybe your friends'll
Send some flowers.

His wife took a paper
And went around.
Everybody that gave something
She put 'em down.

She raked up a Hundred
For her man that was dead.
His buddies brought flowers.
A funeral was had.

A minister preached —
And charged Five
To bless him dead
And praise him alive.

Now that he's buried —
God rest his soul —
Reckon there's no charge
For graveyard mold.

I wonder what makes
A funeral so high?
A poor man ain't got
No business to die.

MADAM'S PAST HISTORY

My name is Johnson —
Madam Alberta K.
The Madam stands for business.
I'm smart that way.

I had a
HAIR-DRESSING PARLOR
Before
The depression put
The prices lower.

Then I had a
BARBECUE STAND
Till I got mixed up
With a no-good man.

Cause I had a insurance
The WPA

Said, We can't use you
Wealthy that way.

I said,
DON'T WORRY 'BOUT ME!
Just like the song,
You WPA folks take care of yourself —
And I'll get along.

I do cooking,
Day's work, too!
Alberta K. Johnson —
Madam to you.

MADAM AND HER MADAM

I worked for a woman,
She wasn't mean —
But she had a twelve-room
House to clean.

Had to get breakfast,
Dinner, and supper, too —
Then take care of her children
When I got through.

Wash, iron, and scrub,
Walk the dog around —
It was too much,
Nearly broke me down.

I said, Madam,
Can it be
You trying to make a
Pack-horse out of me?

She opened her mouth.
She cried, Oh, no!
You know, Alberta,
I love you so!

I said, Madam,
That may be true —
But I'll be dogged
If I love you!

MADAM'S CALLING CARDS

I had some cards printed
The other day.
They cost me more
Than I wanted to pay.

I told the man
I wasn't no mint,
But I hankered to see
My name in print.

MADAM JOHNSON,
ALBERTA K.
He said, Your name looks good
Madam'd that way.

Shall I use Old English
Or a Roman letter?
I said, Use American.
American's better.

There's nothing foreign
To my pedigree:
Alberta K. Johnson —
American that's me.

MADAM AND THE RENT MAN

The rent man knocked.
He said, Howdy-do?
I said, What
Can I do for you?
He said, You know
Your rent is due.

I said, Listen,
Before I'd pay
I'd go to Hades
And rot away!

The sink is broke,
The water don't run,
And you ain't done a thing
You promised to've done.

Back window's cracked,
Kitchen floor squeaks,
There's rats in the cellar,
And the attic leaks.

He said, Madam,
It's not up to me.
I'm just the agent,
Don't you see?

I said, Naturally,
You pass the buck.
If it's money you want
You're out of luck.

He said, Madam,
I ain't pleased!
I said, Neither am I.

So we agrees!

MADAM AND THE WRONG VISITOR

A man knocked three times.
I never seen him before.
He said, Are you Madam?
I said, What's the score?

He said, I reckon
You don't know my name,
But I've come to call
On you just the same.

I stepped back
Like he had a charm.
He said, I really
Don't mean no harm.

I'm just Old Death
And I thought I might
Pay you a visit
Before night.

He said, You're Johnson —
Madam Alberta K.?
I said, Yes — but *Alberta*
Ain't goin' with you today!

No sooner had I told him
Than I awoke.

The doctor said, Madam,
Your fever's broke —

Nurse, put her on a diet,
And buy her some chicken.
I said, Better buy *two* —
Cause I'm still here kickin'!

MADAM AND THE CENSUS MAN

The census man,
The day he came round,
Wanted my name
To put it down.

I said, JOHNSON,
ALBERTA K.
But he hated to write
The K that way.

He said, What
Does K stand for?
I said, K —
And nothing more.

He said, I'm gonna put it
K — A — Y.
I said, If you do,
You lie.

My mother christened me
ALBERTA K.
You leave my name
Just that way!

He said, Mrs.,
(With a snort)
Just a K
Makes your name too short.

I said, I don't
Give a damn!
Leave me and my name
Just like I am!

Furthermore, rub out
That MRS., too —
I'll have you know
I'm *Madam* to you!

JUKE BOX LOVE SONG

I could take the Harlem night
and wrap around you,
Take the neon lights and make a crown,
Take the Lenox Avenue busses,
Taxis, subways,
And for your love song tone their rumble down.
Take Harlem's heartbeat,
Make a drumbeat,
Put it on a record, let it whirl,
And while we listen to it play,
Dance with you till day —
Dance with you, my sweet brown Harlem girl.

TELL ME

Why should it be *my* loneliness,
Why should it be *my* song,
Why should it be *my* dream
    deferred
    overlong?

ADVICE

Folks, I'm telling you,
birthing is hard
and dying is mean —
so get yourself
a little loving
in between.

PASSING

On sunny summer Sunday afternoons in Harlem
when the air is one interminable ball game
and grandma cannot get her gospel hymns
from the Saints of God in Christ
on account of the Dodgers on the radio,
on sunny Sunday afternoons
when the kids look all new
and far too clean to stay that way,
and Harlem has its
washed-and-ironed-and-cleaned-best out,
the ones who've crossed the line
to live downtown

miss you,
Harlem of the bitter dream,
since their dream has
come true.

BLUES AT DAWN

I don't dare start thinking in the morning.
I don't dare start thinking in the morning.
If I thought thoughts in bed,
Them thoughts would bust my head —
So I don't dare start thinking in the morning.

I don't dare remember in the morning
Don't dare remember in the morning.
If I recall the day before,
I wouldn't get up no more —
So I don't dare remember in the morning.

HARLEM

What happens to a dream deferred?

Does it dry up
like a raisin in the sun?
Or fester like a sore —
And then run?
Does it stink like rotten meat?
Or crust and sugar over —
like a syrupy sweet?

Maybe it just sags
like a heavy load.

Or does it explode?

INDEX OF TITLES

INDEX OF FIRST LINES

Grateful acknowledgment is made for permission to reprint previously published poems:

EMILY DICKINSON:

Harvard University Press: Poems number 47, 341 (1 line), 405 (5 lines), 507, 529 (7 lines), 584 (5 lines), 952, 974 (1 line), 1035, 1096, 1198, 1222, 1287, 1406, 1448, 1644, and 1715 from *The Poems of Emily Dickinson* edited by Thomas H. Johnson, Cambridge, Mass.: The Belknap Press of Harvard University Press. Copyright 1951, © 1955, 1979, 1983 by The President and Fellows of Harvard College. Reprinted by permission of the publishers and the Trustees of Amherst College.

Houghton Mifflin Company: Poem 1455 from *The Life and Letters of Emily Dickinson* by Martha Dickinson Bianchi. Copyright 1924 by Martha Dickinson Bianchi. Copyright renewed 1952 by Alfred Leete Hampson. Reprinted by permission of Houghton Mifflin Company.

Little, Brown and Company, Inc.: Poems number 341 (12 lines), 405 (11 lines), 529 (13 lines), 584 (11 lines), and 974 (7 lines) from *The Complete Poems of Emily Dickinson* edited by Thomas H. Johnson. Copyright 1929 by Martha Dickinson Bianchi. Copyright renewed 1957 by Mary L. Hampson. Reprinted by permission of Little, Brown and Company.

ROBERT FROST:

Henry Holt and Company: "The Pasture"; "Mending Wall"; "The Death of the Hired Man"; "After Apple-Picking"; "The Wood-Pile"; "The Road Not Taken"; "Birches"; "Fire and Ice"; "Dust of Snow"; "The Runaway"; "Stopping by Woods on a Snowy Evening"; "The Need of Being Versed in Country Things"; "Fireflies in the Garden"; "A Minor Bird"; "Acquainted with the Night"; "Two Tramps in Mud Time"; "Design"; "Unharvested"; "The Bearer of Evil Tidings"; "A Considerable Speck"; "A Young Birch"; "Directive"; "Forgive, O Lord"; and "The Draft Horse" from *The Poetry of Robert Frost,* edited by Edward Connery Lathem. Copyright 1916, 1923, 1928, 1930, 1936, 1939, 1947, © 1967, 1969 by Holt, Rinehart and Winston. Copyright 1936, 1942, 1944, 1951, © 1956, 1958, 1962 by Robert Frost. Copyright © 1964, 1967, 1970, 1975 by Lesley Frost Ballantine. Reprinted by permission of Henry Holt and Company.

LANGSTON HUGHES:

Alfred A. Knopf, Inc.: "Aunt Sue's Stories"; "Dream Variations"; "Tambourines"; "The Weary Blues"; "Sylvester's Dying Bed"; "Bad Luck Card"; "Water-Front Streets"; "In

278   ACKNOWLEDGMENTS

Time of Silver Rain"; "Winter Moon"; "Suicide's Note"; "Vagabonds"; "Luck"; "Lover's Return"; "Miss Blues'es Child"; "Stony Lonesome"; "Life Is Fine"; "Still Here"; "Blue Monday"; "Homecoming"; "Ballad of the Girl Whose Name Is Mud"; "Little Old Letter"; "Cross"; "Share-Croppers"; "Uncle Tom"; "Song for a Dark Girl"; "Mother to Son"; "Merry-Go-Round"; "Ballad of the Man Who's Gone"; "Madam's Past History"; "Madam and Her Madam"; "Madam's Calling Cards"; "Madam and the Rent Man"; "Madam and the Wrong Visitor"; "Madam and the Census Man"; and "Harlem" from *Selected Poems of Langston Hughes* by Langston Hughes. Copyright 1926, 1927, 1942, 1948 by Alfred A. Knopf, Inc. Copyright 1942, 1947, 1951, 1954, © 1955, 1959, 1966 by Langston Hughes. Copyright © 1970 by Arna Bontemps and George Houston Bass. Reprinted by permission of Alfred A. Knopf, Inc.

Harold Ober Associates, Inc.: "Early Evening Quarrel"; "Juke Box Love Song"; "Tell Me"; "Advice"; "Passing"; and, "Blues at Dawn" from *Montage of a Dream Deferred* by Langston Hughes, published by Henry Holt and Company. Copyright 1951 by Langston Hughes. Copyright renewed 1979 by George Houston Bass. Reprinted by permission of Harold Ober Associates, Inc.

WALLACE STEVENS:

Alfred A. Knopf, Inc.: "Bantams in Pine-Woods"; "Earthy Anecdote"; "In the Carolinas"; "The Plot Against the Giant"; "Valley Candle"; "Disillusionment of Ten O'Clock"; "Sunday Morning"; "Anecdote of the Jar"; "Life Is Motion"; "Peter Quince at the Clavier"; "Thirteen Ways of Looking at a Blackbird"; "The Death of a Soldier"; "Lunar Paraphrase"; "The Idea of Order at Key West"; "The Brave Man"; "Gray Stones and Gray Pigeons"; "The Reader"; "Anglais Mort à Florence"; "On the Adequacy of Landscape"; "Contrary Theses (1)"; "God Is Good. It Is a Beautiful Night"; "Flyer's Fall"; "Debris of Life and Mind"; "Thinking of a Relation Between the Images of Metaphors"; "The House Was Quiet and the World Was Calm"; "Vacancy in the Park"; "Song of Fixed Accord"; "The Planet on the Table"; "Not Ideas About the Thing but the Thing Itself"; and "A Postcard from the Volcano" from *The Collected Poems of Wallace Stevens* by Wallace Stevens. Copyright 1923, 1931, 1935, 1936, 1937, 1942, 1943, 1944, 1945, 1946, 1947, 1948, 1949, 1950, 1951, 1952, 1954 by Wallace Stevens. Reprinted by permission of Alfred A. Knopf, Inc.

WILLIAM CARLOS WILLIAMS:

New Directions Publishing Corporation: "Mezzo Forte"; "The Revelation"; "Pastoral"; "Apology"; "Pastoral"; "Tract"; "El Hombre"; "Mujer"; "Love Song"; "Good Night"; "Danse Russe"; "Smell!"; "The Young Laundryman"; "To Mark Anthony in Heaven"; "The Late Singer"; "Complaint"; "Complete Destruction"; "Waiting"; "The Widow's Lament in Springtime"; "The Great Figure"; *Spring and All* #XIX, "This is the time of year . . ."; *Spring and All* #XXII, "So much depends . . ."; "The Sea-Elephant"; "Poem"; and "This Is Just to Say" from *The Collected Poems of William Carlos Williams,* Vol. 1, 1909–1939, by William Carlos Williams. Copyright 1938 by New Directions Publishing Corporation. Reprinted by permission of New Directions

ABOUT THE AUTHOR

The author of books and essays about American poetry and fiction, JOEL CONARROE is president of the John Simon Guggenheim Memorial Foundation, which awards fellowships to artists and scholars. He has previously served as chairman of the English department and dean of arts and sciences at the University of Pennsylvania and as executive director of the Modern Language Association. A member of the board of directors of PEN, he is chairman of the National Book Foundation, which administers the National Book Awards. He has earned degrees from Davidson College, Cornell University, and New York University, and has been awarded honorary doctorates by several institutions.